The Trail of the Mountain Folk: *A Solo Journey Along the Mountainous Spine of Asia*

OLI FRANCE

www.oliverfrance.com

A Special Thanks:

This journey would not have been possible without the support of numerous companies, schools and individuals who, for some bizarre reason, believed in my outlandish idea just as much as I did. They pitched their support – financial or otherwise – and granted me the opportunity to attempt this journey. For this, I will be eternally grateful.

My thanks go out to Malcolm and Angela Graham of Brickstore, Wigan, Barry Greening of In Touch With Bricks, Lowe Alpine (for the wonderful rucksack), Smaller Earth (A Liverpool-based travel company), St. Marie's RC Primary, Wigan, and Platt Bridge Community Primary, Wigan, and all those who supported me via my crowdfunding campaign: Emma France, Tony France, Anita France, Sam France, Jess Rotherham, Dorothy Atherton, Mary Atherton, Mike Atherton, Mick Kavanagh, Lynda Kavanagh, Mike Kavanagh, Kay Kavanagh, Tony Kavanagh, Carolina de Almeida, Kathy Blackledge, Dave Blackledge, Susan Burns, Dawn Davies, Peter Davies, Sunil Limbachia, Carol Limbachia, Mike Burns, John Richards and Jo-Ann McStravick.

For Emma, and all those who helped me on my way.

1

My promotion was the final straw. I had watched, over the years, as my university friends each became encumbered by the same affliction. This affliction was chasing me too, yet for several years I had managed to avoid its tempting bait. I'd travelled all over the world in search of adventure: trekking with Berbers, dodging bombings in Beirut, and partying with Ugandan army generals. Yet, after returning home in 2013 with my guard at rest, I was seized by that evil vice, and I became a kitchen salesman. So began my two-year ordeal under full-time employment.

I yearned that one day I would escape this curse, but my enemy persisted. I was given a good salary for a respectable job in a growing business, a company car, free fuel, a laptop and a phone, a desk at home with limited pressure from my boss, a bonus and pension scheme, paid holidays and corporate events with all expenses covered, along with opportunities for personal development. It may sound a dream for many, but such trauma for *myself*, I had not foreseen.

As time went on, and after the aforementioned promotion, the disparity between my employment benefits and my ability selling kitchens widened. During twelve months on the road I sold nothing but a single kitchen, only mustered at a bargain price and to a customer with whom I was very well acquainted: the customer being myself. Fortunately, this meant that my career was doomed. And so, after 24 months of hardship, I threw off my guise as a young, astute professional, quit my job, and concluded that my only route back to excitement, was through an adventure.

During this revelation, I had failed to consider some important facts. I, with my fiancée, Emma, were midway through the major renovation of our first home in Wigan, and our wedding was less than a year away. Further, I didn't have any spare money, and I didn't know where to go. Then, a month into unemployed bliss, I developed a knee ligament injury while on a twenty-two mile romp around the Yorkshire Fells.

***

November 2015
Three months later, the Lancashire countryside was beset by a stark autumn breeze. White Coppice is the tiniest of rural villages,

comprised of eight cottages and a wonky cricket ground, now dormant for the winter months. A copper-coloured stream winds into the village from the old mines in the northern hills, where hobbled, at this moment, myself, hand in hand with Emma. I had managed two miles today; a personal best since the injury.

Emma's cheeks were red with the cold as she looked at me, her expression tentative. We had been together for more than eight years, since high school. I love her. Yet for a reason I've never understood, there occasionally comes an urge for adventure which forces our separation. It is perhaps borne from agitation. An agitation which grows exponentially between trips, enhanced by the mundanity of normal life, increased by fond memories of journeys past, driven by future dreams and only cured by foreign exploits. Hence the daily stench of fuel, the traffic jams, inconsequential meetings, isolation, repetition, tedium, dissatisfaction, forced conversations at dismal Christmas lunches, and the countless hours invested into a cause I did not believe in and did not enjoy; had all urged me into a miserable state. The familiar tonic of whimsical freedom had therefore seduced me like never before, and so I knew that on this particular day in the Lancashire countryside, and by the look on Emma's face, and with the inception of an audacious idea, that an uncomfortable moment was nigh.

'Six weeks, eight at most,' I guessed. 'That's all I need.'

Emma frowned at her feet. 'Where do you want to go?'

'Well, erm -.' Emma sighed, then I performed my pitch. 'I want to travel from Hong Kong to Istanbul along the mountainous spine of Asia. If you look carefully at a map of Asia, countless mountain ranges interconnect, from the jungles of South East Asia, across Tibet and into Central Asia, then through Persia, along the Caucasus and into Northern Turkey. Well, I want to travel along all these mountain ranges by any means, meet different mountain communities along the way and climb at least one mountain in each country.'

Emma stopped. 'But, Oli, you can't walk.'

I looked down, sheepish about my leg.

'When do you want to go?'

'In six weeks.'

'I don't know how you can afford it; how *we* can afford it.'

'Okay,' I said, 'if I can raise the money, I'll go. If I can't, then I'll stay.'

Emma shook her head, understandably tired of my stupid schemes. 'You should go. Eight weeks though. No more.'

In the subsequent days, I calculated two things. First, that I would need around £4000 to complete my journey. Second, that eight weeks was a preposterous underestimation for a journey of 8000 miles across an entire continent. On reflection, I might have scrapped the idea upon this realisation, but my plan had already taken root.

This root-taking phenomenon requires some explanation, for it renders my normal human functions redundant. Recently, I had started to build a window seat in our living room and I became so obsessed with every detail of the design that when out for dinner with Emma, I would pause conversation and stare with such severity that Emma may have thought me struck by rigor mortis. I cancelled plans with friends and barely left the house for two days until my project was complete. Likewise, the idea of travelling the breadth of Asia was lodged, and so I knew that my mind would spin until my valiant return to Blighty. I set my departure date for early January 2016, seven months before the wedding, and got to work.

Through Britain's heritage of adventure and discovery, there remain today a number of societies and foundations who work to encourage exploration of the lesser-known world. Biologists, geologists, anthropologists, adventurers and beyond may apply for funding from these organisations in return for new-found information or world-first journeys. These organisations seek proposals which are logical, considered and plausible. I was unsettled by my letters of rejection.

I did experience one moderate success, as I was invited to make a five-minute pitch in Liverpool to convince a group of donors to contribute £500. It was a pleasant evening which placed me one cup of coffee in the black, though my talk only drew the following words of encouragement:

'Nice presentation, but we're just not sure about your project. Maybe you'll come up with one which makes more sense.'

My next publicity drive was to write to regional newspapers: 'PRESS RELEASE: Local adventurer [me] to journey across the mountains of Asia, reaching one summit in each country while documenting the mountain communities...'

I received a phone call from a paper who urged me to: 'Contact us again as soon as the expedition is complete.'

With four weeks to go until my departure, I consulted my expedition finances. They stood at -£15, owing to return petrol to Liverpool. I figured I had lost a few nights in a Vietnamese hostel, which I thought bearable. Meanwhile, I had visited several knee specialists, doctors and physios who concluded that my proposed expedition was nothing but imprudent, and that prolonged rest would be a much wiser idea. They did, however, advise a number of stretches and prescribe some specialist insoles and some strong co-codamol painkillers.

Things were going badly. With every failure or rejection, I envisaged the ominous duty of returning, wage-cap in hand, to the life I hated: a disinterested lay-about unable to flog a kitchen. This vision was my final motivation.

I filmed a promotional video, started a website, branched out on social media, wrote to local schools, outdoor clothing manufacturers and travel companies, started a crowdfunding campaign and contacted notable adventurers. Things started moving and the process became a full-time job.

The four-week caffeine-induced whirlwind earned me two school partnerships, four brand sponsors, crowdfunding success, a free rucksack and a multimedia contract, and ended with me standing in my underwear, ironing sponsor logos onto my t-shirt ten minutes before my ride to the airport.

It was only as I was soaring towards Hong Kong, upset at leaving Emma behind, that I realised how much my fundraising efforts had overtaken my expedition planning. I was without any guidebooks or maps, and my passport was absent of several important visas. Nonetheless, I was flying with a one-way ticket towards the other side of the world, knowing little of what lay between Hong Kong and my finish line, Istanbul, except the exciting prospect a great adventure.

2

My grandmother once said of me: 'If he fell in the canal without a coat, he'd come out dry.' I don't know whether I've found more fortune than other people, but my life to date doesn't seem one of great adversity. I don't mean to paint myself as a wastrel. I've earned my money when I've needed it, but have always tended towards excitement over boredom; a trait which has brought many interesting moments. The very simple philosophy I carry is that *everything will turn out alright*. As I disembarked in Hong Kong airport, I upheld this notion.

Instantly: wonder, colour, charm. The feeling of entering a new land was familiar, if now a little distant. I'd studied Outdoor Leadership at University, and spent my summers and beyond working, trekking and travelling to different parts of the earth. I became addicted; the world my drug. Each journey felt more intrepid. In turn, I became more courageous, or more reckless. I sought the sensation of my t-shirt bouncing from my beating chest. The sense of uncertainty, of danger, of discomfort. I sought the sharp injection of adrenaline to make my mind race, or the ecstasy of reaching a mountain summit after a knife-edge ridge. Each time I ratcheted myself up these degrees of risk and rapture, the more I thirsted for it. For the extraordinary. And so I searched for it. Across four continents and countless journeys, in villages, wild cities, forgotten jungle trails and abstract mountains which lie off the map. I could feel the hit as I stepped off the plane. The latent cogs of exhilaration began to churn. My adventure had begun.

I whizzed among and below the islands of Hong Kong, emerging in the curiously named district of Mong Kok. I saw it already. The racing rhythm of life. The energy. The excitement. Mong Kok, plastered with neon signage, is said to be the most densely populated district anywhere on the planet.

I'd been greeted on arrival by my old friend, Banksy (not of graffiti fame). He led me through a coded door between two shoe shops, up a lift and into his thirteenth floor apartment which overlooked it all. Far below: a pulsating horde of humans, like a troop of ants, bustling, hustling, as dense as the street was wide. I could have watched them for hours, but Banksy had other plans.

We bought beers in a local bar and reminisced about our

school days, before moving on to the plan for my journey ahead. Banksy took notice when our conversation arrived at China. He looked at me, eyes curious as always, and ginger hair bright among the neon glow. 'It's not like Hong Kong, you know. You won't see many other travellers where you're headed in mainland China, and don't be surprised if you struggle to reach Tibet. I've heard that the eye of the state is never far from foreigners in that part of the world.'

I nodded, keeping the thought in my mind, but quite unconvinced that Banksy's warning might prove true. 'So, tomorrow?'

'I'll show you the real Hong Kong.'

It was exactly what I wanted to hear.

Hong Kong is amassed from some 263 islands, home to bronze age discoveries, second world war relics, old fishing villages, country parks, woodlands and reservoirs, and of course, most famously, more skyscrapers than any city in the world. It's a punchy, brazen, and progressive metropolis, which I instantly fell in love with. I could understand why Banksy, the lovable, charming eccentric that he has always been, was mesmerised enough to remain here after our childhood in Wigan.

While walking through a neatly manicured park on the island of Kowloon, Banksy offered an intriguing history lesson. We stood on the former site of Kowloon Walled City. Its title is deceptive, for there were no perimeter walls here, but the city block had the appearance of countless apartment towers which had been trampled by a giant and compacted into an inordinately small space. As would occur if this happened, pipes, signage and wires sprung from every crevice, stairways, alleys and tunnels were formed in obscure places, and living spaces were so jumbled and diminutive that they seemed distorted.

A former Chinese military base, The Walled City became an unofficial Chinese enclave after Britain took control of Hong Kong in 1898. In the subsequent decades, China asserted no effective rule over the city, nor did the British occupants. The city reputedly became a haven for drugs, gangs, prostitution and Chinese spies - entirely off-limits for local police - yet its population burgeoned. At its peak, in 1987, some 33,000 people lived in the ramshackle city block. Several years later, the Hong Kong government demolished the site, tearing open an organic, inventive microcosm, a termite's nest, re-homing its residents and replacing it with a city park. Only old images and Banksy's tale could bring it back to life for me, but I understood why the Walled City has so entranced writers and filmmakers across generations.

The next day, we travelled to Lantau Island, bound for Hong Kong's highest accessible peak; a mountain famous for its glorious sunrises, which left us saturated with mist. It was just a short limp to the summit of Lantau Peak (934m) where we took in the fog, myself dizzied by an unhealthy dose of painkillers. The climb was by far the easiest I would face, but it was a small victory nonetheless.

My initial onward plan was to travel directly into mainland China, then down into Vietnam, before re-entering China from somewhere in South East Asia. Unfortunately, due to some bureaucratic complications, I was only issued with a single entry Chinese visa. Instead, the next day, bidding farewell to Banksy, I made the short flight to Hanoi - saving my Chinese visa – ready to continue overland from there.

It was upon arrival in Hanoi, Vietnam, when I was reintroduced to the common hostel; mythically a refuge for the unwashed and impoverished, but actually a mesmerising base for budget travel. In our modern society, the notion of sharing a bunk-filled bedroom with a group of possible criminals where nought is promised but a meagre breakfast, is more a prison than an accommodation option.

Largely, I am a great proponent of the hostel, though a few unwritten rules can enormously improve one's experience. First, if possible, select a bottom bunk away from the toilet, with a plug socket in convenient reach. Second, this being a public space, the ill-timed removal of one's trousers could amount to a criminal offence. Third, invest in earplugs and an eye-mask or else train one's body to operate without sleep. Fourth, train one's body to operate without sleep as a precaution, in case of early-risers, late night drunkards, excessive snorers, loud traffic, broken air conditioning, broken heating or stinking toilets. Fifth, and lastly, despite the comparable size and smell, this is not the London Underground and other human beings may be spoken to.

My stopover in Hanoi cost the handsome sum of £3 per night, after negotiation. Eager to head straight for the mountains, I spent only one day in the capital, visiting various interesting museums. I am ashamed that despite my cultural exploration, my most poignant revelation in Hanoi was my so-called *Chopstick*

Conundrum theory. I made this revelation (derived from similar issues with celery) as I settled in a local café over a bowl of beef and noodle soup. Through my complete incompetence in the use of chopsticks, it was impossible for me to consume enough noodles to replenish the calories lost through attempting to eat noodles. Simply, one expends more energy attempting to eat, than one gains from eating: *the chopstick conundrum.* I bought a pizza instead.

Vietnam, I thought, is roughly shaped like a sausage, both ends of which have exploded, the northern end more so. On the western side lies Laos and Cambodia. To the east is the South China Sea. To the south, Ho Chi Minh City (formally Saigon), and the sprawling Mekong River Delta. Hanoi sits in the middle of the northerly sausage explosion, and Sapa, my destination, lies in Vietnam's rugged far north-western corner. Here lie the highest mountains in the Indochinese subcontinent, including Fansipan, the highest of them all, and the reason for my journey.

I rose before dawn to catch a bus to the mountain village of Sapa. There had been a thick mist about ever since I arrived, and as we left the city it did not yield. Any hope of spying the distant mountains faded, and I instead watched local farmers working the land with giant buffalo, and rice workers performing their morning chores in the paddy fields. I was only a few hundred miles from Hong Kong's metropolis, yet the pace of life could not be more different. I liked it.

It took seven hours to snake up mountain passes and reach Sapa. The town centre is not overly beautiful, but colour is added by the enchanting ethnic minority women who decorate every street corner with their vibrant handicraft wears. Like most upland parts of South East Asia, Sapa is home to a medley of ancient mountain cultures. Here, Hmong, Yao, Giay, Tay and Pho Lo, plus countless sub-sects, fill the villages of the valley. Traditionally, these communities rely on rice farming in mountainous areas, along with occasional hunting. Today, since a moderate tourist boom in the town of Sapa, many women have turned to craft making, while the more remote ethnic villages offer home-stays. It seems a sustainable trade, though as often happens when tourism finds a poor area, negative practices like begging and high-pressure sales can be a problem. Happily, though, I was only offered smiles and good humour, especially when I joined in with a local football match in the town square. Later, to add an extra smile to the day, I read a sign in a tourist office window: 'Join our walking tour tomorrow. Eight Persons still missing.' I opted to refrain.

I found a hostel, bought some food supplies, packed for the following day and found a spot in a foggy courtyard. My orientation should have ensured a direct view of Fansipan. I waited for an hour, hoping for a glimpse, but the roving clouds only thickened. Measuring 3143 metres, Fansipan is a reasonable one-day challenge, noted for its dense jungle trails, tricky navigation, high levels of rainfall and near permanent cloud. It would be the first sizeable hike of my journey, and the longest trek since I had injured my knee. The coldness in the January air and the mystique of the unseen jungle mountain added a foreboding sense to a quiet evening.

Rising early the next morning, I took a taxi to the remote Tram Ton Pass at 1900 metres, the trailhead for the mountain. It was windswept, barren, and seemed to be plagued by the same saturating mist which had followed me across Asia thus far. There is little here but for a few ramshackle huts and a gateway, through which stands a bleak concrete building with a large front room. In no more than ten seconds, I was summoned into the building by a stern young park ranger, told I could not climb Fansipan, and left to watch my taxi pull back onto the road to Sapa and drive away. The ranger, clean-shaven and clothed in a sharply pressed green uniform had held out his hand and requested my papers. I told him I didn't have any. He looked over my shoulders and asked to see my guide. I shrugged, and he replied.

'No permit, no guide, no Fansipan.'

The speed and severity with which he delivered his verdict left me little opportunity for persuasion. I did try, for a few minutes, to change his mind, but the ranger did not waver. He ordered me to go back to Sapa, find a guide, get a permit, and return tomorrow.

The episode initially left me feeling discontent. Paying to access wild places feels wrong and diminishes the sense of freedom one expects to find there. Some months later though, a news report made me reconsider the reason for this local regulation. I read about a British backpacker who sadly got injured, went missing and died when attempting to climb Fansipan alone. Hundreds of people were involved in the search, and it took several days of traipsing through dense jungle to locate his body.

I managed to hitch a ride back to Sapa aboard a cargo-truck, after a long wait on the pass. Once there, I spent two hours being directed around various offices until I encountered a stern-faced lady who would prove my judge, jury and executioner. I told her what I needed; a guide and a permit. She pulled a few faces, moaned a bit, and said '$75.' With no other options, I agreed.

I planned to meet my executioner later that day to go over the particulars, namely paying the money I owed. In the meantime, I explored a nearby hillside Hmong village named Cat Cat. Away from the hawkers on the street, I'd wanted to grasp the true character of the local ethnic people. I was alone as I trudged down a steep path through the village. The midday showers persisted and fog lingered in the mountains. The tinkling of cattle bells, muffled words from wooden houses, churning of sewing wheels, crowing of cockerels, and the pervasive scent of smouldering fire created an atmosphere of warmth and community: a comforting antidote for a rainy day. Yet no insight could be gained, and little seen, except the occasional shadowed face in the shuttered window. Today, this mountainous corner of Vietnam seemed wholly subdued into lethargy. Tomorrow, I hoped, would bring more.

3

To the alarm of any fire safety officers, many hostels lock their external doors overnight. So after rising at 5am for second attempt on Fansipan, and finding nobody in reception, I was forced to make a clumsy escape through a tiny window. Throwing my rucksack through first, I proceeded to crawl headfirst through the orifice until my trousers got caught on the window latch and revealed to any watching cameras the glowing buttocks of a Caucasian fugitive.

Shortly, I was greeted on the street by a shy twelve-year-old boy on a tiny scooter. He asked, in a squeaky voice, whether I was climbing Fansipan. I told him, 'Yes, I'm just waiting for my ride.' Inauspiciously, he pointed to the back of his scooter.

The boy reserved his only helmet for himself, and ensured I was awake by driving into every pothole along the way. It took some forty minutes to complete the ten-mile journey back to Tram Ton Pass, where my mountain guide was waiting. He, a few years older than my chauffeur, was a modest Hmong man named Ji. I presented myself once more to the park ranger, this time guide at my shoulder, papers in hand, and he allowed us to pass onto the brooding trail.

Ji wore a thick jumper and scarf, along with steel-toed work boots, which looked a few sizes too big. He carried a traditional wicker basket on his back, supported by two rattan shoulder straps. He was short, slight and undiscerning, yet he bolted like a rocket. I jogged after him, recalling some warnings from my executioner that Fansipan normally takes two or three days to climb. I had only one. The route curved down into rich primary rainforest, and followed a laden stream, before jolting up a steep scrambling section and eventually onto an exposed ridgeline, coated entirely in micro-bamboo. We passed only one other guide and his client, who was waddling through the fog in tight double denim. I offered a compassionate nod. The air was thinning, but Ji's pace did not relent. He was born in and built for the mountains.

Lungs busted, I reached the summit in five hours with the emotion of sudden and genuine joy. I couldn't remember the last time I'd had such a feeling. It was the highest mountain I had climbed in a couple of years and proof to myself that I could bypass the residual soreness in my knee to achieve my aims for the expedition. From this day on, I vowed, no pain, difficulty, or physical barrier would stop me. I stood atop Indochina, but I felt on top of the world. I had achieved my aim for Vietnam, but one thing remained uncertain in my mind. It would be, on the summit of Fansipan, that I would find a resolution.

I had been trying to figure the Hmong character for three days, with no certain clues until now. After taking a couple of summit photos, I found that Ji, shivering with cold, was stooped behind a rock and digging through his wicker basket. I knelt and offered him a spare jacket. Hands clasped and with broken English, he politely refused. I stayed beside him and watched as he removed some plastic sheeting, used for keeping the contents of his basket dry. He folded them and placed them down. Then, Ji wiped away the dirt from a flattish rock and laid out a simple cloth. After more careful searching, shivering all the while, Ji produced a baguette, some cheese, a couple of hard-boiled eggs, a tomato and a banana. He placed each item on the cloth, washed his hands with water from his canister and proceeded to slice the bread, cheese and tomato then peel and slice the eggs. Pausing to warm his whitening hands, he beckoned for me to eat.

It may be wrong to make assumptions of all, based on the actions of one, but Ji's humble acts voiced independence, consideration and kindness. I thought of what I knew about the Hmong culture: millennia old small communities bound to the mountains, pushed from China, and from Laos, under times of oppression, and still staunch in their simple existence. Ji wished to take nothing from me, yet he also yearned to give. Rightly or wrongly, I felt that his acts were indicative of a culture which is self-sufficient, yet modestly selfless. After my hesitation, Ji encouraged me again to eat. I split the bread, and we ate together.

The descent was a long trudge into darkness, but on our eventual return to the Ranger's station, I was puzzled to be awarded a certificate, medal and can of cola for my efforts.

Early the next morning, I caught a crowded local bus towards the Vietnamese border town of Dien Bien Phu. I spent the first three hours of the journey with my knees squashed against my chest and beside a pungent old lady who enjoyed spitting in a translucent bag. I got talking to a Vietnamese TV producer on the row in front, who, interested in my journey, reconfigured the seating arrangements to allow me to sit beside him, which kept me occupied for the remaining six hours.

Merely a sprawling commercial settlement, Dien Bien Phu would purely serve as a stopover on my journey. Though an evening wander into town made for a nice encounter with a family of shopkeepers who watched with immense pride as their young son, Ming, served and conversed with me in enthusiastic English.

Again I left at sunrise, bound for a remote border post named Tan Trang on the highland frontier of Laos. From previous travel, I had become wary of overland border crossings with their recurring cons and complications. Unlike entering a country via an airport, border outposts can be a great attraction for corrupt border guards, swindling money-changers, gang-run townships and all kinds of crooks and chancers. As I was to learn during the length of my expedition, my concerns were well justified. Today, Tan Trang's protectors enforced a number of ridiculous bureaucratic levies. Along with the visa fee: a stamp fee, tourism fee, weekend overtime fee and, most outlandishly, a body temperature checking fee. All this was further sweetened by the unfair US dollar/Laos Kip exchange rate offered by the venturesome gents.

Nonetheless, a few dollars lighter and with the sun finally emerging over South East Asia, the bus continued into the wild green valleys of Northern Laos and towards the dawn of an enchanting journey. I arrived in the small village of Muang Khua, located on a bend of the Nam Ou River. Myself and a few other travellers were handed our rucksacks from the roof of the bus. Shortly, I was approached by a cool Polish lady with jet black hair, tie-dye trousers and a cigarette in hand. Her name was Adiyana. She introduced me to her bespectacled boyfriend, Casper, and we were joined by a nonchalant Frenchman from Marseille, named Damien. So we united as a travelling foursome, and I was happy for the company.

A local hostel owner led our group over a pedestrian suspension bridge, along a dirt track and to a row of simple wooden bungalows which overlooked the river. I roomed with Damien, and we soon went to explore the village.

I'd seen Damien earlier, shrugging his way past the Tan Trang conmen. He carried a swagger which made me think he had done all this before. I asked if this was the case.

'Non! Zis is my first taim outside of Oorop. I 'ave a special status in France. My job is at ze Festival D'Avignon; festival of ze arts. But zere is no work in ze winter time. My friend, ee ask if I come to Cambodia wiz him for two weeks. But I do not catch my plane 'ome, and I stay 'ere for two monts. I love it 'ere. De girls, *zey*, zey are amazing, and every night I 'ave been *driiinking, driiinking.* But too much drinking in 'Anoi. So I come to Laos - to relax.'

Despite this announcement, we soon found the only bar in the Muang Khua, bought two beers, and overlooked a river scene of fishermen retrieving their daily catch.

'So, where next?' I asked.

'Maybe I stay 'ere. Maybe I go souz by d'river. Maybe I go nord. I am French; I do not 'ave a plan. And what about you, Olee?'

I explained my journey, before continuing, with an odd French twang in my voice, 'I wanted to climb the highest mountain in Laos – Phou Bia – but it's off limits, covered in unexploded bombs from the Vietnam war. There are thousands of mountains here in the north, but since the war nobody dares go there. These bombs still kill dozens each year. It's too dangerous. I don't really have a plan either, but I can't leave this country until I've found a mountain to climb.'

'Zen, Olee,' he said, eyes flashing, 'I will come wiz you! We will climb ze mountain togezer!' I laughed, and we shook hands to confirm the plan.

The next morning, along with fifteen other travellers and a few locals, we gathered alongside a simple wharf on the river, ready to travel south. The wooden narrow-boat docked beside us looked only large enough for around ten passengers, so people began jostling for position. Yet I can commend the local boatmen for their fight to lower carbon emissions, as they squeezed all twenty-five people, along with luggage, into the solitary vessel.

The five-hour journey offered both spinal pain and magnificent views. We crossed trundling rapids, riverside villages and smiling fishermen. Yet the landscape provided the greatest splendour. The Nam Ou carried us deeper into an empty quarter of Laos, inhabited by sleeping mountain giants, hued from grey karst rock, then topped and surrounded by dense rainforest. The further we travelled, the larger these giants grew, and most passengers were struck silent through awe.

I became hypnotised by this pristine highland, yet on staring closer at the jungle, I recalled its dark secret. For nine years of the Vietnam War, after North Vietnam forces swept through the jungles of Laos, the American military engaged in a prolonged airborne siege of the country. An average of one bombing mission every eight minutes, for nine years, buried Laos under some two million tons of explosives: the equivalent of 158,102 London buses. Of these, up to thirty percent of bombs and mortars did not explode, meaning there are up to eighty million pieces of unexploded ordnance remaining in the Laotian countryside, rendering much of it off-limits to this day. I wondered then, as I stared into the virgin forest, whether, despite the continued woes of local people, this dire legacy of war had paradoxically prolonged the pureness of the jungle.

Our destination was the tiny village of Muang Ngoi, accessible only by boat. For a couple of days, we each became ensnared by the paradise around us. All stress and urgency vanished. One morning, we climbed to a nearby cave, which wound hundreds of metres deep into the mountainside. For a time, we turned off our torches and stood in sheer blackness and total silence. If it wasn't for the ground beneath my feet, I might well have been drifting through the cosmos, as time's flow became immaterial, and the absent signs of life were betrayed only by my beating heart.

Further inside the cave lay a tiny Buddhist shrine, used by sheltering villagers during the bombing raids of the war. Nearby, we found a tiny tunnel, part blocked by branches. Feeling adventurous, Damien and I climbed past, while the others retreated to daylight. We scrambled onwards until we came to a muddy platform over an endless void into darkness. A dropped stone took several seconds to strike the ground. Our platform was perhaps merely wedged over emptiness, yet somehow it felt like no danger could find us here in Muang Ngoi. We felt no fear.

Later, we emerged to music, dancing and the whiff of a camp fire. A group of friendly locals invited us to join them. They shared their beer and food, and we swayed and sang together through sunset and beyond. The next day, with Adiyana and Casper, we made a long trek to the distant Huay Bo village, Damien often visiting the bushes with a stomach problem. Here we found the most peaceful little idyll, where chickens and livestock wandered free, children played with rattan footballs and elastic bands, and hunters wandered intrepidly into the bush with long, homemade rifles.

Meanwhile, dawn and dusk brought time to rest in hammocks beside the river, and evenings entranced us with Laotian cuisine. The three days I spent in Muang Ngoi felt an eternity, and all too willingly, were it not for my sole objective, I may have stayed here forever.

I knew that my gradual journey south would bring flatter plains, and less chance for a mountain climb. Though surrounded by peaks, the Muang Ngoi area is especially beset by unexploded ordnance, as attested by the countless deactivated bombs lying around the village. So, with some reluctance, Damien and I left the others behind and made a short voyage south to the village of Nong Khiaw. We were hungry for a challenge.

'Wow,' said Damien, peering past me as we approached the village. 'Look at zat!'

I turned and viewed a true forested monolith, which formed an imposing sentry over Nong Khiaw on its waterside plateau. 'This could be our mountain,' I replied.

'It may take a long time,' Damien pondered, 'but I suppose, we are in no 'urry!'

Once in the village, we found another wooden bungalow for a few pounds a night and then drifted into an enchanting Buddhist temple. It lay among some jumbled dirt roads and houses, but stood, as all temples here do, resplendent, white, gold and peaceful. We spent a while browsing the main temple and its detailed carvings, before I felt a presence drifting towards us. It was an elderly Monk, placid and meditative, who ambled step by step, eyes upon on us, until he drew to a halt, crossed his palms and said, 'Hello, my name is Tongsi.'

We shook hands and introduced ourselves. I asked Tongsi whether Nong Khiaw was his hometown.

'I was born north of here.' His eyes glistened, and he spoke with an engaging smile. 'It was in Luang Prabang where I became ordained as a monk; all novices dream to study there. Since then, and for twenty years, Nong Khiaw has been my home. You are going to Luang Prabang next, yes?'

'Yes,' I replied.

'And you came from the north?'

Damien and I looked at each other. 'Yes,' we replied.

Ever smiling, Tongsi bowed his head. 'There are many more tourists these days. Yet there is little to do in our village. You are both young, and you are fit. I used to be young and fit too,' he chuckled. 'If you like, I can offer you a suggestion.'

'Please,' I replied, curious.

Tongsi took his walking stick, on which he had been leaning

all the while, and aimed it over our heads. 'Phou Nang None,' he said. 'That is the mountain of Nong Khiaw.'

'Ah!' said Damien, 'zat is ze mountain we want to climb.'

'Is it possible?' I asked.

'Yes,' said Tongsi, 'but you must be careful. The jungle is dangerous. From the edge of the village there is an old hunters trail which directly leads to the top of the mountain. But it is thin, and very bushy,' he chuckled once more. 'If you find the trail, then you will reach the summit. Good luck, and nice to meet you.'

Our meeting was over. As gently as he had approached, Tongsi retreated, and Damien and I were left feeling uncertain but intrigued.

'Olee,' said Damien, as we left the temple, 'I zink we should climb ze mountain tomorrow.'

'We must,' I said, feeling a strange connection to Phou Nang None. 'But today, let's see if we can find out more.'

We trawled the local hostels, tour operators and tourist information spots, before going online in an Indian café. Not a single person could tell us anything more, and the sole line of information we found was on a local website. Like Tongsi had suggested, the website told of an old hunter's trail which leads to the summit. Our question was, come daybreak tomorrow, and in a vast, thickly forested mountain where deadly bombs remain, could we find the trail?

Along my southward journey, the heat and humidity of day had been intensifying, and the next morning we set out into flawless dawn sunshine. Our spirits were high. Damien and I felt well rested, and well equipped; three litres of water stowed in each of our rucksacks. It took a while of searching to find any kind of path, but what we found was a narrow track leading to an old viewpoint. Although not the elusive hunter's trail we were looking for, we opted to get a head start on Phou Nang None. The initial climb was steep and offered a glimpse of what lay below the jungle canopy.

The ground was a wondrous creation of limestone spikes, hollows and caves, each coated in razor-sharp edges. Above this, a layer of crumbling earth, then brush, thorny bamboo, creepers, vines, ferns, lavish saplings and colossal trees. Birdsong was scarce and animal life unseen. But for spiders, insects and the present pair of panting travellers, the forest seemed deserted. After an hour or so, having spotted no direct lines up Phou Nang None, we emerged atop the viewpoint. It was located on a small sub-peak. From here to the actual summit lay a slight saddle, before a steepening mountainside, occasional cliffs, and the eventual peak. Phou Nang None towered: blasé, watchful, goading. I stared back, humbled yet resolute.

It was mid-morning now, and the sun was intense. 'Olee,' said Damien, 'what do you zink? We 'ave reached ze viewpoint and I 'ave not seen a path up ze mountain. Maybe zere is no way.'

I tore my gaze from Phou Nang None. 'Let's continue. The viewpoint path continues along the saddle and down to reach another road. Maybe the hunter's trail lies along there.'

'Yeas, but,' Damien pondered, 'I'm not sure about zis, Olee. You 'ave boots and trousers. I 'ave shorts and trainers, and I am always slipping.'

'If you like, you can head back to Nong Khiaw. I don't mind continuing alone.' I felt cruel saying it.

Damien took a glug of water. 'No, no, no, I cannot do zat. We should stay togezer.'

I nodded, but my thoughts were slightly distant. I felt at that time that bringing Damien with me was foolish. Energised and eager, I felt like rampaging alone up the mountain, but I couldn't bring myself to do it. 'Let's go and find this trail then.'

So we continued, further into the jungle, surveying every opening as a possible trail. Eventually, half an hour later, we found one. Cloaked in leaves it was clearly untrodden for some time, but its bearing aimed directly for the summit. With Damien's approval, we began the climb.

After an hour of slow but careful tracking, the trail completely dissipated. We were left facing stark jungle, with nought to cut a path but a four-inch bushcraft knife. This is where we should have turned back.

4

We climbed on for four hours, using dangling vines to help us scramble over jagged limestone boulders. The dry earth slid beneath our feet, and the prickly fingers of every bush caught us like prey. The vilest obstacles were the vast expanses of near impenetrable bamboo, each piece of which was coated in miniscule black thorns which would lodge in our skin each time we brushed past. We could barely walk a few clean yards without having to fight, cut, crawl or clamber. Sunlight ebbed and darkness grew. The sultry stench of plant spores and sweat lingered. Blood crept down our every limb and our final drops of water had long since been swigged. Our progress became so slow that we ascended no more than one-hundred metres per hour. All the while, we played mental chess with the haunting threat of bombs, whose presence perhaps meant that we were the first people to wander here in half a century.

By 4pm, we had just two hours until sunset. Yet, through the captivating words of the old monk, and our toils against hardship, and the occasional glimpse of the mighty Phou Nang None, I was loath to concede. Damien, though, more exhausted and bloodied than me, slumped against a tree. This was more than he had bargained for.

'Olee,' he breathed, 'I'm done. Please come with me.'

'But it looks so close, and I think there's a clear path ahead.' I'd repeated the same deluded phrase five times already. 'I'll go on a little further, then I'll turn round and catch you up.'

I cannot reason what *truly* compelled me to continue but for the daunting object of failure. I cannot remember a time, for as long as I've slogged up mountains, that I've not made it to my destined summit. It was *meant* to be hard, and my tainted psyche believed I was *meant* to go on until I reached the mountaintop.

I heard the occasional slip and snapping branch as Damien descended. Then, nothing. Just me, the jungle, and impending darkness. The trail I had believed I'd seen ran directly into thicker bush. I sliced at the bamboo, again and again, created a small hollow, and pushed my body through the thorny shoots. I persevered: slicing, hacking, slipping, bleeding. It was relentless, unforgiving and the ground was steepening all the while.

The altimeter on my watch told me I was still two-hundred

metres from the summit at 1465m. Getting fatigued and thirsty, my chances were dwindling, and doubts were beginning to circulate. As I paused, breathless and clinging to a vine, I heard movement in the surrounding trees; an animal, I thought, or a hunter.

Then, I heard the familiar call, 'Olee, Olee! I could not leave you here alone. We need to go.'

I took one more upward glance and a heaving breath, then turned back to join Damien. Our descent into twilight proved equally arduous, as we often lost our trail and became disoriented. At one point, I took a slip and stopped on the edge of a limestone cliff. Damien and I stuck together, guided by our solitary torch, until we eventually emerged on the road after nightfall. We were dehydrated and covered in cuts, grazes, thorns, bites and dirt, but we were out of the jungle.

I bought Damien dinner that evening. We sat weary-faced in a dark café, picking at bowls of fried rice and at the thorns in our arms. I felt a real conflict of emotions. Guilt, at leading Damien so far. Thanks, that he'd encouraged my return. Then, in a deeper aspect of my mind, comfort. Not comfort at escaping the jungle, but comfort at the grit I had found to continue for so long through the rainforest. Comfort, that two years spent flogging kitchens hadn't stripped me of my mettle. Comfort, that this lingering quality, however foolhardy or reckless, would probably be the single factor which gets me through my long journey to Istanbul. That is, if it didn't kill me first.

'Olee', said Damien, the next morning, limbs decorated with plasters, 'we look like we 'ave been in a fight!'

I smiled. 'So, will you be coming next time?'

'*next time?*'

'We didn't make it to the summit, so I will have to climb another mountain.'

His laughter provided my answer.

We could not find our bungalow owner, so we posted our keys and modest stipend through a hole in her bamboo shack, and made off for the bus station. Damien and I had decided to continue further south and leave behind the Nam Ou river. We caught a five-hour bus to Laos' historic capital, Luang Prabang.

This deeply religious city lies in the heart of the country and perhaps magnetises more visitors than anywhere else in Laos. I understood why, for it occupies a glorious lowland spot by a bend in the Mekong river, and stands bejewelled in Bhuddist and French colonial architecture. Orange-robed Monks and camera-swinging tourists intermingle on the narrow city streets, among tuk-tuks, traders and teashops. It was mid-afternoon when Damien and I arrived. As we trawled the night market, Damien was ecstatic to find an eatery offering 'Genuine French Baguettes' which very nearly reached his exacting standards. 'Almost,' he said, licking his fingers, 'almost as good as the baguettes in France!'

I had wondered, as we negotiated the modest hamlets of the Nam Ou, whether the sedate tempo of life we encountered would exist across the country. It seemed so. There was a placidness to the Laotian people which caught me by the heart. A contagious tranquillity had entered my body, slowing my very steps. My zest for adrenaline was quelled by my lust for relaxation.

The only notable bar in Luang Prabang is a sprawling oasis, bedecked with palms, lanterns and rhythmic tunes. Its name: Utopia - *an imagined place or state in which everything is perfect* - Laos defined. I drank enough beer to enhance my own state, and considered the dreamland through which I had journeyed. The souls of the village children exuded unbridled joy, untroubled by the burden of materialism or greed. It may sound strange to say I felt envious, but I truly did. I had tasted money, to a certain extent, and my monthly payslips had never sent me frolicking through my village, beaming with uncontrollable delight and dancing with my kinsmen. Yet, a simple elastic band had provided this effect for the children I had watched. Worth, I thought, is the most misunderstood concept of our age. Anyway, the musings of this sozzled stoic received timely vindication the following day.

Damien and I hired a scooter and rode out to the nearby Kuang Si Waterfall, a vast myriad of falls, roaring through the jungle into turquoise pools and plumes of mist. We trekked beyond the selfie-snapping hordes along a lonely forest trail and a down a deep cavern beyond. Here, hundreds of yards below a mountain, we found more Buddhist relics, whose pious faces glistened from the dim corners of the cave. It was dusk when we returned to the park entrance. The tourists were long-gone and the stalls shuttered. Apart from a couple of distant figures, we were the last people there. As we reached the scooter, Damien began tapping his pockets, then digging through his bag, then scratching his head.

'Olee, Olee,' he double-checked his pockets, 'I've lost the

key.'

'Right, erm,' I offered my own pockets a hopeful tap, but the key was missing.

As we pondered our predicament, an elderly Laotian man wandered towards us, from where he had been waiting, and produced, from the pocket of his torn trousers, our misplaced key. Not speaking any English, he pointed to the ignition, where Damien must have left it, before offering a jovial smile, and hobbling home for the day.

'Khob chai! Khob chai! (*Thank you! Thank you!)*' we called after him, but it seemed our saviour sought no appreciation.

'He must 'ave waited 'ere for six hours,' said Damien, disbelieving.

We watched as the old man turned down a forest trail. My heart was seized once more.

In a lucid moment, I realised that Laos was diverting me from my overall journey. It was time to head north. Damien had planned to continue towards southern Laos, but I was happy when he opted to continue a little further with me. We caught a seven-hour bus to the bleak transit town of Oudomxay. A perishing winter chill marked our midnight arrival.

Damien wrapped a newly purchased scarf around his head, and I donned another jacket, as we set out from the lonely bus terminal. A deserted highway sloped towards the town, and a signpost marked the distance as five kilometres. Shivering with cold, we marched on.

The weight on my shoulders made me feel out of shape. At all times I carted two essential bags. My primary pack was a large expedition-style rucksack. In here, I carried all my spare clothing, meagre toiletries, first aid and repair kit, charging cables, then lots of warm winter clothing, plus mountaineering boots, an ice axe, walking poles and crampons. I also carried a thick down sleeping bag, a sleeping mat and a bivi bag (a human-sized waterproof sack, which provides a modest abode in the mountains). My second bag was a lightweight daysack, filled with important documents, cameras, a small, barely-functioning laptop, a constant stash of food and water and my humble notepad. The total weight of my gear amounted to a rather spine-bending 25 kilograms. I wore my large expedition pack on my back, and my smaller pack on my front, to take the silhouetted appearance of a pregnant man ferrying a fridge.

It always takes time to recondition one's body to lug such heavy weight. Two and a half weeks into my journey, the strain remained uncomfortable.

'How far 'ave we walked Olee?' asked Damien, eyes flashing through the gap in his scarf.

I glanced back at the five-kilometre sign. 'Not far, it might take another hour.'

As Damien stopped to fetch another jacket, a trundling tuk-tuk stopped beside us. The driver made an easy sale, and we rattled down into Oudomxay. The north-westerly wind whooshed from the freezing uplands of Tibet, and all in the town was empty and quiet. Leaving the tuk-tuk, so began our long trek through the ghost town: Damien; head-scarfed and tired, Me; anxious and weary. Like Mary and Joseph, we were turned away from three different inns, until an hour of wandering brought us to the walnut door of an old lady, who welcomed us in.

Cocking her eye, but without a word, she fetched a key and led us to a shaded room at the end of a first-floor corridor.

'La ti savad, (*goodnight)*' she bowed, leaving us to rest. The room was a musky box with two beds and nothing more. It seemed long dormant. We hauled the cold blankets over our fully clothed bodies, grumbled at the broken shutters, and fell asleep.

Oudomxay was one of those peculiar towns where, despite its population, there is a slowness and mundanity to life which unsettles the foreign traveller. One feels like an unexpected guest in a silent movie, curiously tracked by the eyes of all its characters. Like so, and as rain began to tumble, we walked the next morning to the local market, in search of hot food. We followed a fleshy stench to find a local lady working an oar-sized spoon through a dark broth. Huddling with locals in a grimy shelter, Damien and I sat over two bowls of the stew. The dank climate had been sapping us of conversation. Instead we sat and contemplated our own affairs. The villagers babbled as the downpour thickened. My chopstick dexterity was improving, and I gorged on a good measure of noodles and meat. We paid our dues and made for the bus station.

'Nex' bus: two hour!' said the ticket-seller.

Damien's charm bought us two cups of Laos coffee and seats around a shopkeeper's fire while we waited. Local travellers wrapped themselves in blankets, towels, and anything they could find to stay warm. The five-hour northward journey intensified the chill, as a frosty wind swirled through the broken windows, yet, as we inched along precipitous roads, it also promised my return to the mountains.

'Hey! My name's Rosie, this is Kate.'

I retrieved my bag from the busboy on the roof, and extended my hand. 'I'm Oli.'

'Damien.'

'Are you heading to Luang Namtha too?' I said.

'Yeah,' Rosie replied, vivacious with her Australian twang.

We shared a cramped tuk-tuk into the village of Luang Namtha, nestled in a triangular plateau and in wild north-western Laos.

'So what brings you guys here?' said Rosie, 'it's off the tourist trail, right?'

'It is,' I replied, 'and it's good to be here. I'm heading towards China on a long mountaineering trip. This is the last place I'll find a mountain to climb in Laos.'

'Isn't that a little, *dangerous*, you know, with all the bombs in the jungle?'

'*Yes*,' Damien interrupted, smiling as he drew from his cigarette.

'Yes, we, erm, ran into some trouble last time. Anyway, how about you?'

'We're going gibbon spotting in a couple of days,' replied Kate, with a clean English accent.

'But if you guys are interested,' Rosie resumed, 'We hear there are a bunch of ethnic villages around the mountains here. Maybe we can go explore them together?'

I was instantly obliged. Damien, casual as ever, confirmed our plan with a shrug, 'why not!'

Our group landed in a charming alpine-style lodge in the heart of the town. The following day, as the rains persisted, we mingled with latent travellers, did research, and made arrangements for our journey into the surrounding townships.

Luang Namtha is located in the infamous Golden Triangle: drugs, hedonism, smugglers, hippy trails and jungle; a mesmerising narrative which has now all but vanished from this rugged corner of Laos. The Golden Triangle, encompassing chunks of Laos, Thailand and Myanmar, was the world's second heroin superpower after Afghanistan. Thousands of tons of the drug once passed from this region into China and across Asia, providing rapture and ruin for centuries. I was fascinated to imagine how this inconspicuous part of the earth was too the harbourer of a forbidden poison. The Laotian jungle was a truly deceptive veil. What remains here now are primitive villages, where rubber and banana trees far outgrow opium. Yet whispers, quantified by UN surveys, imply the resurgence of Laos' illicit crop.

I maintained this thought as my gang and I ventured north the next morning. We had chartered a decrepit minibus and a local guide to show us the rarely visited villages of the Nam Ha Protected Area. Noxious fumes billowed from the air conditioning vents as we drove first to the market town of Muang Sing. I accidentally bought three bananas after a trader mistook my good-morning wave. Rosie reported the ghastly sight of an elephant's foot for sale, and Damien and Kate enjoyed some Laos coffee.

Despite its oddities, this market was a melting pot of Laos' countless ethnic minorities, who each journey here to buy or sell wares, vegetables, meat, fish, currency and handicrafts. Border-hopping Chinese traders arrive to flog cheap electronics to captivated locals and, in a disturbing corner of the market, buy the cut hair of local women to be made into wigs and extensions.

Shortly, we visited a *Khmu* community, Laos' largest minority; a spirit-fearing culture still engaged in practices of magic and fortune-telling. Sacred archways guard the village from storm, flame and evil, and indigenous men remain proficient in hunting and trapping game. On our arrival, the village seemed empty, until the jubilation of a secret wedding found our ears from the village square. Our guide advised us not to intrude. We moved next to an *Akha* village; an egalitarian culture whose people are beautifully clad in indigo dress. We visited a *Yao* village, overrun by playful children, a *Hmong* village, guarded by bow-wielding youngsters, and a rare riverside *Lanten* community, curious of us, as we were of them. We were invited into the roadside restaurant of a Hmong man, who was delighted to show us his kitchen. This included, amongst other morsels, a freshly caught giant jungle rat. We became instant vegetarians.

This experience was timely, partly for exploring Laos' different cultures, but mainly for aiding my mental shift. The Nam Ou River had left me waylaid, yet observing these villages changed that. Children ran, danced and played. Women sewed, flogged produce or worked the land. Men tended to animals, gathered crops or ventured into the forest. People were getting busy. For too long, I had neglected my own busyness. I had always been an arch-enemy of inactivity. It breeds an agitation only cured by a dose of physical suffering. The bustling village scenes awoke me from my Laotian dream with a rigid slap to the face. Stop slacking, I told myself, it's time to climb a mountain.

The prevailing cold had finally bitten for Damien, and he decided to return south towards warmer climes. He left at dawn the next morning, along with Rosie and Kate. Meanwhile, solo once again, I remained in Luang Namtha to confront my unfinished business. China beckoned tomorrow.

I had located a mountain using the GPS on my phone; unnamed, but around the highest in the Luang Namtha basin. I hired a simple mountain bike, bought food, water and a cheap jungle machete, and set towards the mountain. A ten-mile cycle past hordes of waving children took me to the edge of Ban Kok Mee village, where I covertly slipped into the forest and tied my bike to a tree.

I was heartened that this part of the country was far less heavily bombed during the war, yet the jungle was scarcely absent of dangers. Bears, tigers and leopards are all known to exist in this region of Laos. Mercifully, the lower part of the mountain was a sparse but steep rubber tree plantation, which made for good progress. I had heard rumours that some plantation owners are responsible for the hidden opium farms, located in concealed tracts of private lands. Small armies of local people are known to reside in these forests, tasked with collecting the precious white liquid from the hewn trunk of each tree. This liquid is collected in white polystyrene tubs, which just then were blowing in the wind to create an ethereal soundtrack in an otherwise deserted place. They tinkled and tapped with the lick of every breeze. I was following no trail but instead a compass bearing through the linear landscape of this unknown forest. The tinkling tubs continued to sound, and occasional leaves whisked among the tree roots. I started to feel unnerved.

Sighting dense jungle ahead, I retrieved my machete, and continued with caution. There was a distant campsite. Nobody was there. I pressed on, the cover of jungle luring me forward. Deluded or astute, I rotated with almost every step, scanning, inhaling, scanning, inhaling, until, shortly, I met the eyes of another man.

He stood beside a tree 30 yards below me, holding, like I, a machete in his hand. And he stared. I returned his gaze. We each remained motionless, waiting and wondering, until, with a lick of my lips, I yelled, 'Sabaidee! (*Hello!)'*

He tilted his head, his bare toes twitching in the leaves. His clothes were tattered and dull. He raised his machete slightly and replied with one of the few Laotian words I knew, 'Phou? (*Mountain?)'*

I nodded, and waved up the hillside, 'Phou, phou!'

A pause. Then, the young man offered a brief smile and disappeared back into the trees. I let out a breath and loosened the grip on my machete. I'd averted an all but certain fight to the death, and I continued on my way.

The incident did nothing to settle my nerves as I wandered from the plantation into the jungle. Here, I happened upon a vague trail which led through a short section of forest then out onto the edge of a man-made clearing. A site for more rubber trees, I wondered, or for something else?

I'd been climbing for an hour or so when I felt the return of Laos' humidity. When this arises, it is a dense and inescapable force: a sapping thief of all one's energy. I was only a mile from the summit, but my new bearing led directly through unbroken rainforest. I didn't realise it then, but it would be perhaps the slowest mile I've ever walked. I spent three hours hacking paths, hitting dead ends or steep slopes, crawling on my stomach along animal trails, becoming lost, exhausted and on the brink of turning back. Then, sliced and covered in mud, I emerged on a small knoll which marked a nameless, insignificant summit in an uncharted forest, but which at that moment felt like the top of Everest. I stood atop the loftiest tree trunk, stabbed my machete into the air and screamed, 'woooohoooo!'

My adrenal glands released a sharp shot of adrenaline into my blood stream. As it whizzed around my body, sweat burst from my pores and mingled with dirt, my heart erupted, and my muscles seized with victory. Laos' toxic sedative gave way to electrifying euphoria. I was back in the game.

As I cycled away at dusk, I paused for a while to watch the sun set over the mountains, feeling happy and reflective about my lesson in perseverance and looking forward to bigger challenges ahead. It was time to journey from a country of six million into a land of one billion. That is, if I could make it past the border.

5

Nobody was going north. Here marked the boundary of South East Asian backpacker paradise and an unfrequented region of China, devoid of hostels, cheap traveller bars and timeworn tourist trails. From here, my journey would join an altogether separate flow and the promise of unfamiliarity was alluring.

I caught a bus bound for the Chinese city of Jinghong, situated near the southernmost edge of Yunnan province. Getting there meant crossing through a place named Boten: Laos' only open border with China. Once, this town was the opium traffickers favoured route into greater Asia. On the Laotian side, gambling moguls had since opened vast casinos and hotels to cater for a Chinese lust for betting. In 2011 though, such activities were banned by the Chinese government, leaving Boten a faceless ghost town, ruined by the aftermath of debauchery.

We cruised through. I thumbed through my passport to see the promising gleam of my month-long Chinese visa. I had dumped my machete in Luang Namtha, got my papers in order, and felt assured of an easy passage. I was joined mainly by Chinese workers, venturing home for the forthcoming Chinese New Year. Also aboard was an American family: Kris, a doctor, along with his wife and three children, who were working in Yunnan and completing a visa run.

I was stamped through Laos' border post and into no-man's-land. We drove the short distance, to halt at the outstretched palm of a camouflage-clad soldier. He wore a helmet with black goggles, and held a powerful-looking assault rifle at his chest. Two more soldiers boarded our bus and escorted us out. They remained impassive as our bags were scanned through security, before directing us inside the imposing border post.

The process seemed slick. Chinese nationals were stamped through within thirty seconds, then the American family passed through without a hitch.

'Yes,' said the border guard, summoning me with his finger. I placed my passport on his desk and he eyed me up and down. Without a second word, the guard began flicking through each page of my passport, inspecting every stamp and visa. Five minutes elapsed and the travellers queueing behind me were getting restless.

Glancing at me once more, the guard handed my passport to his colleague at the second desk, now holding up both queues for a further five minutes. The bus-lady became animated as she watched from behind the guards, anxious that I was holding up the journey. There was nothing I could do. The border guards made me wait on a nearby bench.

A more senior official arrived shortly and observed me with some severity. He took my passport into two separate offices, before he and the two previous guards confronted me. Only one of them spoke reasonable English. He sat beside me while the others stared. I had seen that the guards had taken a particular interest in two visas. The first: an old American working visa. The second was a Tajik visa scheduled for the middle of March this year, and I understood why it had caught their attention.

The guard cleared his throat. 'Where are you going in China?'

'Just Yunnan and Sichuan,' I lied.

'Have you got a flight ticket to leave our country?'

'I'll buy one in China,' I lied again.

The guard returned, more abruptly, 'When are you going to Tajikistan?'

'Ah,' I offered a lying smile, 'It is a separate trip, *another trip*. I will go home from China, and will go to Tajikistan later, *later*.'

The guards glanced at one another. If they wouldn't let me into China, my entire plan would fall apart.

'Do you have another ID?'

'Yes,' I beamed, able to offer a genuine response. I dug my driver's license out of my wallet and handed it to the guard.

The officer and guards convened for another discussion as they decided my fate. I tried to emit an aura of innocence as other travellers and the impatient bus-lady watched on with intrigue. The guards returned, escorted me to a border desk, asked a few more questions and then dropped, like an executioner's guillotine, their stamp onto my passport.

'*Access granted.*'

A cluster of guards watched me as I scurried after the bus-lady and out into China. I sensed that this ordeal with Chinese officials wouldn't be my last, and the episode left me feeling unwelcome across this strange frontier.

The lush green uplands of Laos were replaced by a stark and dispiriting landscape. Smog brooded on the barren mountains, stripped of forest and fauna. The new watchmen upon the hilltops were power lines and radio towers. Below, the valleys were severed by treacherous roads, beset by foolhardy drivers. Beside them, troops of rigid soldiers guarded bland concrete buildings, and a weary-faced populace gazed forlornly upon their degenerated land. All the colourful contrasts one associates with Asia were starched bland by the unicolor palate of environmental negligence. Had I languished much longer, staring from the bus window and solitary in thought, an irrevocable animosity for China might have taken hold. Yet I was greeted, by the tap on the shoulder, with a timely interruption.

'Hey, buddy, what happened back there at the border?' asked Kris, the American doctor I'd met earlier.

I explained the incident.

'And they were interested in your *American* visa?' he frowned.

'Yeah.'

'Tibet,' his wife said, nodding.

'Yeah, it'll be for Tibet,' said Kris. 'They're really sensitive about that area, especially at this time of year. It's the Tibetan New Year soon, and if you haven't been to China before, they just want to check you out a little bit. Anyway, where're you headed?'

'I'm travelling through Yunnan province towards Chengdu, and then, erm…'

'Chengdu! And how long until you need to get there?'

'About two weeks.'

'Two weeks! And you're travelling by bus.' I raised my eyebrows, unsure of where this was going. 'I think you might struggle,' Kris consulted his wife with a grimace, 'It's almost Chinese New Year. As you can see, people are travelling all across the country to return home for the celebrations. It's known as the *largest human migration on earth*. You're about to join the wildebeest train my friend.'

I returned to thought. My journey across the world's third largest country could span no more than the thirty days allowed by my visa. A largely uncertain route had one guarantee, that I would exit into Kazakhstan through China's most mysterious and sensitive region excluding Tibet: Xinjiang province. I had no doubt that the border guards, on seeing my Tajik visa, suspected that I would be travelling through this far-western region. Back in the UK, I had fashioned a fictitious trip through China in order to collect my visa, for the state is adamant that travellers must not journey through Xinjiang. Now, I left behind a separate trail of lies at the border, which meant that nobody knew my travel intentions. For now, I was happy to keep it that way.

Over the next three days, as I hopped towards the mountains via Yunnan's city transport hubs, unexpected things began to happen. In Jinghong, I was invited to join some locals for a table tennis and tea-drinking marathon. In a crowded Kunming bus station (the unnerving site of a mass killing in 2014), I was chased by female police officer, who was delighted to reunite me with some money I had dropped. Locals helped me use ticket machines and directed me around confusing stations. I was brought complimentary food as street-side cooks endeavoured to satisfy my hunger. Bus passengers offered me the best seats, and shared their overland snacks. I encountered good humour, goodwill, and a charming curiosity in my alien appearance. Against all my initial perceptions, I was starting to see the importance of social duty and hospitality in China. Ever so slightly, this country was drawing me in.

I eventually arrived in the ancient town of Dali, enclosed within stone walls on a plateau between Erhai Lake and the Cang Shan Mountains. Naturally, the latter were the reason for my arrival. This was the far-eastern edge of the Himalayas, where the weighty tectonic plates of Eurasia and India have wrestled for millennia, to produce vast battalions of mountain ranges aligned from north to south in formation. This meant a ruggedness to the peaks, unseen in South East Asia, and my first glimpse of snow. Indeed, the Cang Shan formed an imposing backdrop to beautiful Dali, rising steeply through pine forests to the icy summits above. Though a haze remained, I could spy the scarcely-trodden pinnacle of Zhonghe Peak (4100m): my target for the following day.

Dali was an interesting traditional town: short, squat buildings, with wonderfully-tiled sloping roofs, cobbled streets, oriental wooden beams, and splashes of red from lanterns, bunting and canvas. On a sundown exploration of the town, among hordes of Chinese tourists, I received an enthusiastic greeting.

'Photo, photo!' A Chinese girl in her early twenties rushed towards me. She had a cartoon-character appearance, with oversized glasses, dungarees and a broad cherubic face. 'Photo!'

'Ok, ok,' I said. I was getting used to Chinese strangers asking for a *photo-with-an-Englishman* souvenir. Though odd, I was always happy to oblige. I leaned in for the selfie as she fumbled with her phone.

'No, no, photo – me!'

'Ah, right,' I played it cool.

She thrust her phone into my hand and posed before an ornate archway. 'Ahhh, Thank youuu!' She skipped backed towards me. 'Photo – you, photo -you!' She pointed at my camera.

I glanced around, somewhat bewildered. 'Erm, Ok.'

After a moment's consideration, the girl positioned me before one of Dali's most enchanting relics, the local McDonalds, and I offered an awkward smile.

After snapping more photos than was truly necessary, she returned my camera and declared, 'You're my friend!'

'*Ok*,' I said, half-smiling, half-frowning, 'do you speak English?'

'Lit-tal,' she replied, pinching two fingers together.

We eventually established one another's names, of which hers was Ping, or *Duckweed*, if translated. She insisted on buying me dinner and teaching me the bongo drums in a music shop. I bought her a cake to say thank you. She bought me a cake in return, then gave me a hug and jumped in a tuk-tuk, leaving me mystified on a busy street corner with a cake under my arm. A more peculiar evening I have rarely enjoyed.

'*Danger in the Cang Shan Mountains*,' I read, late that evening, after packing my kit for the climb tomorrow. A guidebook warned of the risk of robbery on solo hikers in Dali's mountains. I could find no information or maps of my desired route. All I knew was that the trailhead begins beside a military base at 1900 metres above sea level. From there, an uncertain 2200 metre ascent beckoned. I dreamt that night that I wandered through a forest. Sharp-eyed bandits began to emerge. They chased me, knives drawn. I ran, and I ran, and then I woke.

It was two in the morning. In my drowsy state, doubts about the mountain, some deluded, others real, began to circulate. For whatever reason, Zhonghe Peak became an omen in my mind. I found just an hour of deep sleep until sun pierced the curtains of my dorm-room. I had overslept – my reliable internal clock confused by an unsettled night. I bought some food and water and made for the trailhead. I was required to sign-in at a quiet ranger's hut, staffed by three loitering officers. Mine was the first name on their list in days. Across the nearby stream, dogs and yelling soldiers could be heard over the concrete walls of the military base.

The rangers watched on as I crept onto the trail. The initial slopes were cloaked in a tranquil pine forest. Solid stone steps guided me through a vast burial ground. Chinese tradition dictates that the deceased should be buried high on a hillside in order that the dead will be at peace. Water-facing slopes, like this one, which glanced towards Erhai Lake, are even more favoured. With a discomforting mist drifting through the forest, I kept alert to any strangers, yet it seemed I was alone.

After the initial ascent, the path traversed the mountain for a mile or so, before reaching a few shacks in the forest. Smoke drifted from a solitary chimney and the place was frequented by a single old ranger. Observing me closely, but saying nothing, he gestured for me to sign-in again, before nodding up a scarcely-trampled path.

I nodded back at him, and his eyes seemed to narrow. Half-an-hour later, as a chill reached the mountain, and snow covered the forest floor, I reached the final building which showed on my GPS. It was a simple stone structure, of four walls and an inner courtyard. The wooden gates were fixed shut by a huge padlock, but a dirty window offered a glimpse inside. I could hear music playing. It was gentle and meditative. Buddhist ornaments and plants lined the courtyard. I peered around the edges of the building, yet once more, the forest was empty.

I pressed on, needing to gain some ground. Soon, the snow revealed footprints: of cats, large birds, deer, bears, and humans. It was a soft and powdery snow which became ever-deeper as I climbed, meaning I had to slog through, rather than atop the surface. The human footprints eventually stopped, and I pursued virgin snow. I was above 3100 metres now. The sapping fingers of altitude were just beginning to find my lungs. It was past two o'clock and I cursed my late start. As I continued, the snow thickened beyond my knees and towards my hips, to slow my every step. When I paused to calculate my time to the mountaintop, I realised that nightfall would reach the summit before I did. Winter's nocturnal chill and my uncertainty of the trail ahead forced me to concede for today. I retreated, angry at myself, but vowing that my dual with the fairy-tale-land of Zhonghe Peak was not over.

To enhance my chances, and with a promising weather window coming, I took a rest day in Dali and became acquainted with a most eccentric band of dorm-dwellers. There was a Chinese mother and daughter who were an excitable pair of shopaholics. Then, a charming old Japanese man on a tai chi pilgrimage, whose dawn ritual of slurping yoghurts ensured everyone was awake. There was a scurrying local lady, who dashed around with an unexplained fervour, and spoke not a word of English. There was myself. Then, there was a young Chinese-Canadian traveller called Michael.

Michael told me, as he arrived that day, wide-eyed and with a pristine rucksack, that this was his first time staying in a dorm room. He was eager to receive a short education in dorm-room etiquette, and I was happy to share my invented commandments.

Yet, in an audacious breach of commandment number one – *Thou shalt not publicly remove thine trousers* – Michael's jeans struck his ankles at the very moment the scurrying Chinese woman burst into the room. She gasped some inaudible phrase and fled, leaving poor Michael to consider his sins.

That night, the Chinese lady, who entertained us all with waffling sleep-talk, left me dumbfounded. Out of her Mandarin babble, she said, in perfect Southern drawl, 'Life is like a box of chocolates, you never know what you're gonna get.'

I was delighted at dawn, when my alarm clock rang and I could exchange this madhouse for the mountains. This time, I reached the trailhead before sunrise, when the rangers station was unguarded. Again, I pursued the stone steps through the cemetery and along the mountain, then past the shacks (vacant on this occasion), and beyond the snowline to find my footprints from two days ago.

Reaching 3500 metres, the powder snow was over a metre deep and the gradient was suddenly steepening. The frozen crust rarely held my weight as the morning sun turned sharply on the mountain. With every step, I sunk to my waist and slipped backwards as the snow gave way. Not my ice axe or walking poles could gain much traction. I tried spreading my bodyweight as much as possible to move along the ice crust, but I crawled and climbed and slipped and fell as though caught in a nightmare where progress is impossible. Infrequent saplings became useful aides, but the further I climbed, the deeper the snow became. It was now around minus 10°C and the effects of altitude were tangible; my full-body exertion begging too much of my divested lungs.

After a sapping eight-hour ascent, with Zhonghe Peak in the near distance, I reached the crux of the climb. Reaching the mountaintop meant traversing thirty metres across a perilously steep slab of snow which had a one-hundred metre run off below. A rudimentary sign warned of danger. The sun was beating against the slab, and I knew that the snowpack was incredibly weak. But I had come so far, I wrestled in thought. The summit was in sight.

Summit-fever coerced me to extend a probing leg. The snow slipped beneath it and a small chunk tumbled downhill. This sight forced my sobriety. I made the decision that traversing the slab alone in these deserted mountains was simply too risky. Fortunately, my efforts were not entirely in vein. At around 4010 metres, Zhonghe's sister peak was just a thirty-minute climb above me. I scrambled out of the sparse forest to see pristine snow-capped mountains all around. I rested for a while after my 2100m ascent, and enjoyed three of China's rarest commodities: solitude, silence and oxygen. They were worth every step.

I ran, slid and skidded down the mountain to reach my hostel just after nightfall, and complete the challenge in thirteen hours. With this, my attention turned immediately to Tibet.

This mysterious corner of the world, whose ancient culture is borne from the world's highest and largest mountain plateau, has entranced me for many years. I longed just to glimpse, to whiff, to experience Tibet's beguiling mystique first-hand. The image of Tibet in my mind, to this point, remained uncertain. What I envisaged was an Eden-like place: slowness, peacefulness, immaculate natural beauty and a divinity which taps into the soul. I was within touching distance of this unfamiliar world, yet the challenge of getting there remained both great and beyond my control.

Geographically, Tibet can be defined in two ways. First, it is a province which stretches little further than its eponymous Plateau, and is named the Tibetan Autonomous Region. Then, traditionally, it is a much greater tract of land, once ruled by Tibet's ancient empire and still inhabited by its descendants. This extends into the provinces of Yunnan, Sichuan, Gansu and Qinghai. To enter the Autonomous Region, foreigners require an entry permit, issued by the state, and they must join a tour group or hire a private guide. Often, all access into Tibet is restricted, and indeed the region has only been open to visitors since 1980. Unfortunately, the costs of the permit and guide were beyond my budget for the expedition. My plan instead was to reach some of the fascinating communities on the periphery of the Plateau, yet a warning came from many sources: *foreigners are not always welcome* (by the state at least), and should I stray into actual Tibet, fines, detention or deportation would await.

Due north was a city whose name oozed the charm I sought: *Shangri-La*. Once, this was a fictitious and mythical paradise, whose location has been disputed by generations of explorers. In 2001, the residents of one Yunnan town decided to overrule all other theories and rename their own town from Zhongdian to Shangri-La, for the reason, a cynic might say, of attracting tourism. Nonetheless, Shangri-La stood as a gateway into outer Tibet, and so I made the five-hour journey to get there.

What I found was a ghost town, perched upon a frozen tableland at 3200 metres. On my sundown arrival, a biting wind reared and the temperature began to plummet. For this reason or another, as I marched into the old town, I found that I was alone. So alone that all lodgings, all cafes, all shops were shuttered. So alone that all streets were utterly deserted. So alone, that even the grand central square, overlooked by an ancient monastery, seemed abandoned.

After an hour of traipsing these empty streets, I came to a long pathway on the roadside. It led through weeds and dying grass towards a murky window, inside which, I saw movement. I followed the path and saw a small wooden sign above the doorway: 'Hoztel.' I raised my fist and knocked. A young Chinese lady answered and the laughter from within paused. Seven faces looked at me, then the laughter resumed.

This was a friendly bunch; a cheerful microcosm into which I had serendipitously fallen. I was ushered beside the stove and given a bowl of hot noodles. Beside me; three female workers, and a couple of their friends, joined by a Ukrainian lady and a Japanese man. The Ukrainian lady, Nataliya, was the only person who spoke English.

She turned to me, and away from the gigging Chinese girls. 'They want to know what you're doing here?'

'I'm hoping to travel to the north, first to Litang, if you know it? I want to journey along the Sichuan-Tibet highway.'

Nataliya translated to the Chinese girls, and the came back, 'why?'

'Tibet,' I smiled.

'They warn that this road is sometimes closed to foreigners, and that it may be covered in snow at this time of year. It crosses many high mountain passes.'

I was aware of this, and the thought worried me. I had planned a very important rendezvous in Chengdu for which I could not be late. This highway was by far the most direct route, and the *only* route through Tibetan villages. 'I can only try,' I mused. 'Why is it so empty here?'

'Nobody lives in Shangri-La, they tell me. It's a tourist town, but no tourists come here in the winter because of the cold, apart from us, I suppose. So everybody else leaves – the hotel owners and the shopkeepers. It is very strange. There is little for us to do here now, but if you like, the girls said they will show us the town tonight.'

I finished my noodles, added another coat, and we trooped out into the town. The central monastery, *Guishan Si*, was now a golden beacon below the night sky, floodlit from all sides. Beside it stands the world's largest prayer wheel, at twenty-one metres tall, which required our entire group to rotate it. It happened that a friend of the Chinese girls owned a local bar. Although closed for the winter like everywhere else, the owner unlocked the doors, dusted down some glasses, poured us each a beer and played us his guitar. Perhaps Shangri-La's residents were not entirely wrong to rename their city.

The next day, I travelled with Nataliya to the bus station. I was hoping her Mandarin might help me acquire the northbound bus ticket I needed. We arrived at the desk and Nataliya translated to a vigilant ticket seller. Nearby, a police officer was watching, cigarette in hand.

'Ticket to Litang,' said Nataliya.

The ticket-seller glanced at me. 'No bus today.'

'Xiangcheng?' I asked, (a town en route to Litang).

The ticket-seller shook her head, 'No bus today.'

She was lying. I knew it. Public transport runs like clockwork in China. Buses do not cease to exist.

Using Nataliya's Mandarin, we started to probe and question, 'When is the next bus? Why no bus today? Are there any buses to the north?'

The ticket-seller glanced past us, and the police officer

reached our side. He leaned in and repeated, with smoke on his breath, *'There is no bus.'*

6

With no reason to remain in Shangri-La and unable to continue north, I found myself on a southbound bus towards the town of Lijiang, feeling discontent. My new route towards Chengdu was a colossal detour which would push me further from Tibet. Yet, with Chinese New Year on the horizon, I longed that my about-turn might prove fortuitous.

Lijiang, I learned, was once the favoured holiday haunt of China's super rich. If Venice had a birth-child with quintessential China and Disneyland, it would be Lijiang. It is a fabulous if outlandish town, with waterways, and twisting cobbled paths through an 800-year old miniaturised metropolis. Trees and greenery occupy rare spots in the town and giant waterwheels gyrate before the flash of camera lenses. Every building is an open-fronted tourist delight, offering musical instruments, toys, local foods, souvenirs, and festive finery.

The super-rich trail-blazed for the inordinate Chinese middle-classes who, upon my arrival, seemed hell-bent on frisking my every body part. Never have I experienced such human congestion. And yet, for an hour I trudged through this frightening legion with twenty-five kilos of rucksack and only a vague idea of where I was going.

Once thoroughly violated, I was spat from the vortex and through the doors of my desired hostel, which felt at once an oasis.

'Welcome, my name is River.' The owner was a mild-mannered and instantly likable man.

I asked if he had a bed for a couple of nights.

'Of course! We are very quiet at this time of year.'

I could hardly conceive how.

River showed me to a well-constructed dorm room, whose only occupant was a friend of River's, named Johan. 'If you don't mind me asking,' I said, 'How is it that your hostel is so quiet, when it's so crowded on the streets?'

'Ah,' said River, 'Chinese New Year is a strange time of year. The foreign tourists stay away because it's too busy. But Chinese tourists love it here in Lijiang, only they prefer to stay in hotels. But I'm happy with that, I can enjoy the holiday too.'

'And what will you do to celebrate?'

'You know that it's New Year's eve tomorrow. In the evening, myself and Johan, with our friend, Robin, will share a traditional dinner and toast to the new year. You can join us if you like.'

I was hugely grateful for the invitation, which I humbly accepted.

I spent the next day enjoying Lijiang's wondrous spectacles: fireworks, costumed dancers, festive music, well-wishers, exploding firecrackers, and most delightfully of all, a local man walking his llama.

As the evening arrived, I sported my finest attire (some jeans and a t-shirt), and was greeted by River, Robin, Johan and a mammoth spread of food. Robin had produced an array of fish, prawns, pork, noodles, rice, ribs, exotic vegetables, wonderful salads, and most importantly, a hand-made selection of dumplings. I had not witnessed such a feast in weeks, and I swallowed to conceal my salivation. Outside, party-goers were rushing along the street and ceaseless fireworks provided the musical backdrop to our banquet.

We discussed all manner of things: travel, sport, economics, our hometowns, before our circuitous dialogue arrived at China's great taboo. By now, beer and wine had been free-flowing; relaxing, perhaps, the politically-watertight lips of these Chinese acquaintances. I told them about my inability to reach Tibet. 'Do the Tibetans not have a right, like the rest of China, to receive tourists freely?' I asked.

Johan, my most loquacious companion, replied, 'Well, Oli, I am very...*liberal*. And I have visited Tibet myself. I do not think it is fair, but the situation is very complicated.'

'Do you mean to say, it is an uncomfortable subject?'

Johan lulled his head, his drunken eyes spinning in thought. 'Imagine this: you have taken control of a huge area of land, whose people are accustomed to an ancient culture, very different to your own. Then, you wish to make your country into a global superpower. But Tibet had become quickly restless, which you might understand. Its residents did not want to change their culture. They did not want to yield to the State. The problem for China is that no country ever became great when it was plagued with such internal conflict. So China had two options, release Tibet from its possession, or repress it. Until Tibet is indistinguishable from China, in culture and language and education, the situation will remain the same.'

'Ok,' said River, placing a hand on Johan's shoulder, 'let's not be serious. It's New Year!'

Johan nodded. He wiped his mouth and raised his glass, and we crashed our beers together, 'Ganbei! (*Cheers!*)'

At midnight, we followed ritual and shared the dumplings, before offering many rounds of good-wishes for the year ahead. Robin disappeared for a moment, before returning with a petrol canister and four tumblers from the kitchen.

He tapped the canister, 'Baijiu from my village: rice spirit. sixty-eight percent!' He poured four glasses of the dubious stuff and put an end to all subsequent memory.

After rediscovering my coherence later the next day, I came up with a plan. I had some time to spare until I needed to reach Chengdu, so I decided, upon the encouragement of my Chinese friends, to trek through the legendary Tiger Leaping Gorge. For three days I did so, venturing into one of the world's deepest gorges, which at its greatest depth measures almost 4000 metres from the Jinsha River below to the towering Jade Snow mountain above. Along the way I joined with an Australian, a Korean, an American, a Dane, a Belgian and a Dutchwoman, to complete the United Nations hiking society.

The magnitude of this cavernous valley was beyond anything I have ever witnessed.   Its river, solely fed by the mountainous basin, roared terrifyingly past house-sized boulders. Only four people have been imprudent enough to attempt to raft this river. None of them were ever seen again. High on the gorge's lofty shores exist a number of small Naxi communities. This scarce ethnic minority is one of Yunnan's oldest, and by my own experience, one of the most welcoming.

Offering a blip of contrast, our hiking society reached a guesthouse on the second day ran by an angry and deplorable witch, named Tina. Her wrath, I eventually found the funny side of, it being so permanent and unfounded. Guests and staff alike would quiver in her restaurant domain, as she hurled abuse and venom towards the meekest of recipients for the humblest of crimes, like not raising one's hand immediately upon the delivery of one's meal.

After tiring of Tina's pantomime, our troop decided to venture to a lesser-explored corner of the gorge, named Walnut Grove. This was the final hamlet on the tallest perch. We trekked through the sapping heat of day along a dry and dusty road to arrive in a Naxi utopia. We became the day's only customers in a simple eatery, ran by the most ancient, miniscule and friendly old lady, who was so delighted to see us. Her diminutive face and hands sprouted from an oversized red coat, and a large woolly hat protected her head. She spoke in the sweetest voice, which set her face aglow along with ours, and we were charmed by the hand-etched wooden menu, which offered 'Noddles,' rather than noodles.

After returning briefly to Lijiang, I boarded a 24-hour bus bound for Chengdu, in anticipation of my important engagement. The journey was made instantly unpleasant as a travel sick girl on the seat in front released a pool of vomit onto the floor below. I arrived in Chengdu with two revelations. First, that I have never been to country in which urinating is such a fiercely expensive pastime, with toilet hawkers praying on every call of nature. Second, that sitting down continuously for 24 hours causes infinitely more back pain than trekking with a heavy rucksack, proving, in a short experiment, what humans are truly designed for.

My reason for venturing away from the mountains and into China's fifth largest city was for the brief visit of my fiancée, Emma. Having taken five and a half weeks to cover a quarter of the distance from Hong Kong to Istanbul, it was clear that my prediction of a six to eight-week trip was badly inaccurate. Our wedding was now just six months away, and progress had slowed on our house renovation ever since my departure. During quiet days on my trip, I was coordinating electricians and builders, and speaking to wedding photographers and bands. Then, during slow days, I missed Emma. This is the travellers taboo. Every gap-year or sabbatical-taking nomad who traverses the world in search misses home, if they have a home to miss. Yet this does not fit with the outward portrayal of constant joy, and the upheld belief of greener grass on distant shores. I had travelled alone for long periods before, but this was when Emma and I were still young.

Now, nine-years into our school-time romance, we were virtually living together, and were about to get married. We had seen each other almost every day for the past three years. There were times where all I wanted was to hold her delicate, soft hands, and to feel her head against my shoulder, and to kiss her. I reflected on her life at home without me: worrying about my safety, consumed with a house renovation, wedding plans and a full-time job, and *alone*. Alone without the occasional exhilaration which gave balance to my emotions. And every time I gave this thought, I felt immense guilt. Yet I was concerned.

I worried that bringing Emma to China, despite yearning to hold her and to see her, could be a mistake. What if being in her company once more would make it impossible to continue when I became alone again? Through prolonged isolation, one's mind becomes a fickle beast. I could not reason, until the moment Emma emerged from the airport, whether this would be for better, or for worse.

Then, we were together, and doubts instantly faded. We were together, as though our separation was but a fleeting dream. Emma and I trekked up Qingcheng Mountain, visited a panda reserve, and explored countless local tearooms, monasteries and markets. We fell in love all over again. But then, in a flash, she departed. Emma left me in a cold street in Chengdu at dawn, with these final teary words, 'Oli, we belong together, not apart.'

Solitude returned.

I had already bought my onward ticket for the same day, knowing that to linger in Chengdu would be foolish. I needed instant focus. I therefore fixed my aim on making a second assault on Tibet. I was embarking on a two-day journey to the Tibetan village of Langmusi, a fabled heartland of ancient Tibetan culture, home to sky burials, ancient monasteries and surrounded by a mountainous colosseum. Adding further enticement, the sacred Tibetan New Year festival was due to take place on the day of my planned arrival.

Eight hours north-west of Chengdu lies the Tibetan frontier town of Zoige, which sits on a windswept plateau at 3500 metres. I had entered a bleak and unforgiving landscape. A frozen gale whisked across the tablelands, pushing the temperature towards a twilight low of minus 20°C. Tibetan nomads braved the weather and wandered the deserted streets, attired in thick yak-wool chubas (traditional coats). I made straight for the bus ticket office; a hole in a ramshackle hut.

'Tashi delek (*hello*). Langmusi, tomorrow?'

The young lady behind the desk looked shy and uncertain. She turned to her colleague and they spoke briefly. The lady translated a message on her phone, then showed me the screen. '*No bus tomorrow.*'

I smiled to myself, I ought to have expected this. I tried again, 'Langmusi, tomorrow, bus,' I pointed at a bus. 'I know, I know,' I tapped my head. Then I tapped my watch and held up seven fingers to indicate the time of its departure. 'Tomorrow.'

Bashfully sinking into her coat and smiling at her colleague, the lady simply shook her head and pointed once again to the message on her screen. This was agonising. I knew beyond doubt that there *would* be a bus tomorrow. Unwavering online timetables had assured me of that. I was angry. I had travelled for eight hours into another freezing ghost town and was being told that I could not continue. Moreover, I had just eight days to travel more the 3,000 kilometres through some of China's most sensitive regions, before my visa expires and I'm collared by the local cops.

I went to the shop to buy some food supplies, before returning as dusk fell, and seeing the ticket-seller walking home from the station. 'Please,' I held my hands together, 'Langmusi tomorrow.'

The lady shrugged her shoulders, smiled timidly, and continued on her way.

In a lucky moment, I was approached by a local lady who, seeing me wandering the town with my rucksacks, asked if I needed a place to stay. I followed her to a very basic guesthouse, perhaps the only one in town, and she showed me into the tiniest bedroom I have ever seen. It was the exact width of the narrow single bed within, and there was just enough room to open the door at the foot of the bed. A window above the bedhead offered unrivalled views into the reception area, and a torn net curtain ensured that privacy was impossible. Yet at these temperatures, I wasn't for getting undressed. The guesthouse owner and her daughter beckoned for me to join them for dinner. We shared rice and a hot vegetable stew, and I was encouraged to 'Eat, eat, eat.'

Thoroughly stuffed, I turned beside the stove and watched a wintry storm blow in after nightfall. I rested with a hot cup of tea, ruminating over my next move, until the front door creaked open and a Tibetan nomad entered amid a flurry of snow. He brushed some snow from his shoulders, shivered a little, and blew into his hands. The nomad settled beside the stove, but did not lift his eyes. We each remained like so for half an hour or more, quiet and contemplative among the bitter harmony of winter's wind.

Then, the nomad raised his head and looked at me. I looked back, and was surprised as he spoke in eloquent English.

'What brings you to the town of Zoige?'

'I'm on my way to Langmusi, but I'm having some difficulty. The ticket-seller tells me there is no bus tomorrow.'

The nomad frowned, 'Of course, that is not the case. A bus leaves for Langmusi every morning at seven.'

'So I believe.'

The nomad continued to frown. 'You know that there is a big festival tomorrow? It is Tibetan New Year: *Losar*. Hundreds of people will be going to the village of Langmusi to celebrate at the monasteries. I hope that you may see it.'

I nodded, *'Are you going to Langmusi too?'*

'No. I'm visiting home for the festive season. My village is not far from here.'

'And where have you come from?'

The nomad paused and glanced at the stove. 'I work in New Delhi.'

'New Delhi?' It seemed a strange workplace for a Tibetan nomad.

'Yes, I have lived there for the last ten years. You see, I work the Free Tibet Press. I am a journalist. However, we are not allowed to operate inside China, and now that I have come home, I am under watch.' He paused.

'So, there are people following you?'

'I don't know,' he paused, 'but when I return to China, I must hand over my passport and call the police once a week to report my whereabouts.'

'And what if you wish to return to New Delhi, when you don't have a passport?'

'Well, I must seek permission. Anytime I want to leave my village, I must seek permission. If they do not grant this, then I cannot go anywhere. It is a very difficult situation. Home no longer feels like it did when I was young. There is too much tension, too much discord, and sometimes I feel like I am imprisoned. Since I left home ten years ago, many Chinese businesses have arrived in Tibet. This makes it harder for the Tibetan people to live well. My people must learn Mandarin, but the outsiders do not learn Tibetan, and sometimes our culture feels marginalised. I am sad to tell you that life in Tibet is filled with turmoil.'

I considered the Nomad's words, before his voice returned in a different tone. 'So, you wish to go to Langmusi tomorrow?' I nodded. 'Then meet me here at 6am and I will help you.'

7

I found the nomad by the stove the next morning, gazing into a blizzard. I wore all the clothes I owned. For the nomad, his yak-wool chuba was enough. We set out from the guesthouse and made the short walk towards to the bus station. This cold, in the dead of Tibetan winter, was more intense than any climate I have experienced before. It, like a school of piranhas, gnawed into the flesh.

'Wait here' the nomad told me, pointing behind the ticket office. I gave him some Chinese Yuan. He returned with a ticket in his hand and a smile on his face. 'There is your bus,' he pointed to an old vehicle, whose engine was already chugging. Several shrouded faces peered through the windows.

'Good luck, my friend,' said the nomad, extending his hand, 'and remember, you are very welcome here in Tibet.'

We shook hands and I thanked the nomad before slipping onto my bus. Shortly, we ventured from the shelter of the town and along an exposed plateau road. Wind and snow formed mesmerising patterns on the deserted highway ahead. Inside the bus, the faces of Tibetan locals portrayed intense introspection, and moments of euphoric stupor. Inertia overcame their bodies, except for the whirling prayer wheels in their hands, and the devout hum of their rumbling lips. Outside, the wind was shrill. Snowflakes whistled around the cabin as passengers released prayer flags through open windows. Meanwhile, I remained still amongst them all, entranced by the beating chords of Tibet.

The bus halted and its door screeched open. I followed a corpulent old nomad onto the roadside. A roaring wind tugged his hair and clothes, but he marched on, his mantra unbroken.

From here, a narrow side-road twisted for three miles into Langmusi. Where this road bent in the distance, I spotted a police checkpoint lying in wait. The old nomad flagged down a passing car. I thought he was oblivious of me, but he turned and encouraged me to follow. The driver and his passenger were Buddhist monks. Beside me, the old nomad continued to chant; his prayer wheel spinning and spinning. I buried my head into my coat and we cruised past the first checkpoint. Langmusi came into sight; a white and gold wonderland surrounded by snowy mountains. We passed a second checkpoint, this one more substantial than the last, with a large riot vehicle blocking half the road. It seemed I had gone by unnoticed.

Then, Langmusi awaited. I thanked the driver and continued alone. I found a room for the night in a creaking wooden guesthouse, but only stopped to leave my bags, for a swarm of marching people had seduced my attention.

They drifted uphill towards a distant monastery. All ages walked. From young novice monks with shaven heads and ruddy cheeks, to timeworn old ladies, faces gnarled by the Tibetan winter. I joined their troops, and all people alike said, 'Hello.' As we continued, open trucks full of worshippers were arriving in the village. Frozen bodies inched onto the roadside and converged with the pilgrimage. We passed below a golden archway and into the older part of town. Kerbside cooks fried an array of festive treats as lofty bellows pierced through the smoke and snowstorm from beyond.

I followed a separate group of men, old and young, towards a small monastery across a stream. There I found a billowing chimney, and a group of female worshippers outstretched on the ground in reverent prayer. Other pilgrims circumnavigated the monastery, as the group of men climbed a nearby hill, from where the screams and bellows came. I pursued them up the slope, where, plagued by ceaseless snow but inspired by pure delight, they hurled prayer flags and breathless howls into the blizzard, crying for good fortune for the year ahead.

These flags swirled with the snow, the young men continued to roar and I turned to behold a giant ancient monastery across the valley, where a huge crowd was gathering. Here, the main celebration was underway. Locals formed a deep circle around a central stupa. Periodically, costumed Buddhists emerged from the monastery, some wearing helmets and carrying large spears, others wearing elaborate cloaks and deathly masks. They danced and swarmed and skipped. Beside them, two hundred novice monks observed them, Tibetan longhorns blasted their rhythmic tune, drums throbbed, the crowd chanted, fires blazed, snowflakes fell, the wind whipped and roared, and I watched, eyes agape, the most spectacular thing I have ever seen.

The celebrations continued for 8 hours or more until the sun burned through the blizzard and set the colours of the town alive. During this time, I was constantly mobbed by friendly locals, delighted to host the only foreigner at their proud festival. A group of twenty young men surrounded me for half an hour and asked every curious question they could conceive: '*Where are you from? Are you a Buddhist? Do you like Tibet? Are you warm in those clothes? Do you need some dumplings? Do you have yaks in your country?*'

Interrogation over, we huddled together into nightfall, as the costumed dancers made way for fireworks, bonfires and feasting. When the evening chill returned, I said goodbye to my local companions, and realised that I *really did* need some dumplings, having not eaten all day.

That night, I settled in my sleeping bag as it reached -5°C inside my room. When I dozed among the ongoing fireworks, the dreamland inhabited that day by my body and that night by my mind was so alike in its wonder that I felt adrift in a state of imagination.

Morning brought clarity. The quietness which pervaded Langmusi was unsettling. Gone were the fireworks and the horns and the drums, the chanting, the snowstorm and the hilltop bellows. Gone was the crackle of fire and the worshipful footsteps. All was truly silent. The otherworldly festival was now but a vivid slice of Langmusi's history, embedded only in my mind and in the memory card of my camera. Today, Langmusi again became a quiet Tibetan village in the mountains. Ordinary life resumed. Yet my business here remained unfinished. Indeed, it was the mountains which first enticed me to this settlement, and it was the mountains that formed today's agenda.

I packed my winter gear once more, and breakfasted on a second helping of dumplings from my guesthouse. I took the same route through the village that I had followed upon yesterday's arrival. This time, I walked alone. As I reached the great monastery, a couple of young monks were sweeping away the festival debris. The fires beside them breathed a dying white smoke. I continued past a second monastery, whose encircling prayer wheels stood dormant.

In the distance now, I spied the opening of a narrow gorge, pierced by the stream which splits the village. Here I saw people. There was a group of four ladies, with two children. I caught them as they ambled across the water. Just here, a cave entrance was adorned in prayer flags and the remnants of a fire. I thought back to the cave-shrines of Laos. Beyond the cave, water seeped from where the upper part of the stream was frozen. It was at this juncture where the group of ladies halted. They each knelt towards the freezing stream and washed their hands and faces. This was clearly sacred water.

I walked on along the gorge to reach an expanse of untouched snow, I realised that I was being followed. A little mongrel dog stood behind me, head tilted and eyes wide. He was only small, but had a curious and loyal looking face. He stopped a short distance from me and stared. I named him Nomad.

'Come on, Nomad,' I said, 'you can come with me.'

My target was a mountain named Huagaishen Shan (4200m). There was no marked trail to this summit, but like most of my climbs so far, it felt intrepid, and the solitude was exciting. I was standing in a small snowy basin, surrounded by cliffs on most sides, with a couple of mountain buttresses and thin valleys. Nomad was unwilling to help with navigation, so I opted to climb directly up a slope coated in tough juniper bushes.

We climbed for two hours before reaching a small cliff face, up which we needed to scramble. I went first and waited at the top for Nomad. He looked up at me, paws on the lowermost ledge.

'Come on, Nomad!'

Nomad sat down.

'Alright,' I sighed, 'wait there.'

I climbed back down and tried to help Nomad up the cliff, but he wouldn't let me get near him. He was a stray, unused to human contact.

'I'm trying to help you Nomad, I don't want to leave you here.'

Nomad clawed at the rock before retreating with a moan.

'I'm sorry,' I said, 'I need to carry on, but I'll come back for you soon!'

I climbed back up the cliff and left poor Nomad behind. For the next half an hour all I could hear was the echo of Nomad's barks and cries. After five hours of climbing, I reached the fairly simple summit of Huagaishen Shan, marked by prayer flags, and from there could observe the infinite highlands of Tibet.

The cold was perishing up here, so I turned back after just a short rest. On my return though, I somehow missed my previous trail and began following a steepening snow gulley between two cliffs. At one point, I had no option but to jump ten feet down onto thin pile of snow. My crampon twisted on a rock, and one of its spikes stuck in the calf of my other leg. I went on with dark clouds gathering overhead. The landscape suddenly felt quiet and forbidding. Footprints in the snow reminded me that bears and wolves roam these mountains. My water bottle had frozen many hours ago, my urine was brown and I felt dehydrated, a condition worsened by altitude.

I knew the bearing I needed to take, but now my options were limited to this gulley. I could not safely climb back, nor up the cliffs which surrounded me. I could only go down. It was a slow and nervous descent. I had no ropes, and could use only my crampons and ice axe to descend steep, loose snow and sudden rock faces. In moments like these, one considers all the implications of a fall: there is no mountain rescue here, nobody knows where I am, I have no signal on my phone, the mountains are deserted, and nightfall with its lethal cold is approaching. Yet there is nought like stark danger to bring rigid focus.

I completed the descent after several uncertain moments, and was thankful to reach the snow basin by the frozen stream. Most happily of all, I saw Nomad's little footprints aiming back along the water; he had made it to safety. I passed the sacred bathing area and the cave-shrine to sight the village once more. It was now, as dusk approached, that Langmusi offered me its final spectacle. This time, revealed with the sight of vultures.

Langmusi is one of few remaining Tibetan communities where sky burials are still practised. Tibetan Buddhists hold the belief that when a person dies, their soul leaves the body, rendering the corpse an empty vessel. By offering one's dead body back to nature, a person conducts a final act of selflessness, and in turn completes the circle of life. After a funeral ceremony, bodies of the dead are taken to a holy burial site, usually on a hilltop, their flesh and bones are hewn by a specially trained *rogyopa*, and their remains are left for the vultures and crows. Bones and teeth are ground with flour and fed to various animals, and in a short period of time, all that is left is the soul of the departed, liberated now to be reborn.

And so, the vultures circled over the monastery upon the hill. I walked past, but chose not to encroach any further. This was not to avoid a gory sight, but through the belief that some of Tibet's mysterious practices deserve to reside beyond the realms of outside eyes.

The evening served me with myriad emotions. I had evaded

the grasp of the local law and sensed merriment, delirium and warmth, then tranquillity, sacredness and mortality, each of a great and everlasting order. These two days impelled profound thoughts about my own existence, and how I wish for it to play out. I reflected on this all evening, knowing that I must leave Langmusi the next morning. Yet before I fell asleep, I settled that if nothing else, I needn't ever return to this obscure community, high upon a cold and hilly plain, to recall the eternalised magic of a town named Langmusi.

8

Five men in jeans and jackets loitered on a street corner in the modern side of town. I had seen them from a distance, and they had seen me. It was mid-morning, and my rucksacks were settled on my shoulders. I continued along the opposite side of the street. As I walked past the men, they started to move. I kept my eyes in the distance, in search of the daily bus, but my observers were approaching. They crossed the road and surrounded me.

A squat man with a glowering face showed me his police badge. 'Passport.'

I reached into my chest pocket and handed it to him. Two men continued to watch me, while the others huddled over my passport. Several minutes passed as they inspected the weathered pages. Again, for a reason which remains unclear, they took a particular interest in my old American working visa. A discussion ensued and the glowering man made a phone call. I became tense, but settled that only one tactic might solve my problems. It was time to play the *stupid tourist*.

I beamed at the two men watching over me, 'Ok, ok?' I shrugged and smiled again. One man weakened and nodded at me.

Phone call over, the glowering man turned to face me. He seemed the only one who spoke any English, and only at a basic level. This was good.

'Langmusi, you, why?' he asked.

'Ah!' I smiled, 'the mountains,' I pointed towards the peaks, then tapped my expedition pack and acted like a cheery hiker. 'China mountains very good!' I held my thumbs up.

The interrogator glanced at his colleagues, two of whom were now smiling at me.

I kept up the charade, 'Me, *Yunnan, Tiger Leaping Gorge*,' I nodded at the men and I pretended to take a photo, '*Sichuan, Chengdu.*' I drew circles with my finger to gesture just how expansively I had travelled, before offering my final conclusion, 'China, very good!'

The glowering man remained impassive, scrutinising me and my passport in equal turn. 'Langmusi, you, leave.'

'Yes, yes!' I said, 'I go. I go to Xiahe.'

'Now.'

'Yes, yes, now!' I smiled again.

The glowering man grumbled and shared a word with his deputy. They took some pictures of my passport, placed it back in my hand, and stood aside to let me continue. I shook the hands of my two most cheerful supporters, and hurried along. This felt an uncomfortable moment, and was perhaps a narrow escape, but it was only a small concession for having spent two days in Langmusi.

The bus never arrived. I waited for an hour, under the distant watch of the policemen, until I met two villagers who were also going to Xiahe. We paid a local driver to take us there. It was a four-hour drive through the dusty north-eastern corner of the Tibetan plateau.

'We must take slower route,' said one villager to me. 'The western road is closed to foreigners.'

We were travelling into the southern reaches of Gansu province, where Tibetans, Hui Muslims and Han Chinese reside. The confluence of these cultures could perhaps be pinpointed in my destination. Xiahe has volatile history. Its famous centrepiece, Labrang Monastery was built in 1709 and is the largest place of Buddhist worship outside of the Tibetan Autonomous Region. Ruled since its inception by Tibetans, power struggles of warring clans and outside forces provided two hundred years of unrest. Then, in 1917, Ma Qi, a ruthless Muslim warlord, backed by the Chinese Empire, led his troops through the mountains and into Xiahe. They swiftly claimed Labrang monastery and challenged the Tibetan's resistance against the Empire.

Rage festered for eight long years, until, in a bloody coup, the Tibetan's struck back. Ma Qi, briefly ousted, returned with 3000 troops and brutal might. Monks and villagers were gunned down. The stomachs of the living were gouged and stuffed with hot rocks. The skulls of the dead, be they men, women or children, were strung like garlands upon the encircling wall of the monastery. A town once consecrated lay defiled.

Two years later, upon the reunification of China, Ma Qi gave up Labrang Monastery. His duty of supporting the Empire was complete. What remained upon his departure though was a bitter division between the Tibetans, and the Chinese and Hui Muslim settlers. Further periods of unrest followed in the coming decades after Tibet came formally under the control of the Chinese People's Republic, and Chairman Mao enforced the repressive 'cultural revolution'.

Xiahe only reopened to foreigners in 2012 following more periods of riots, the facts of which are uncertain given China's media restrictions. Yet I knew, upon my arrival, that this unassuming town had more than a short tale to tell.

Regretfully, my foremost impression of the town was of an unpalatable stench. Yaks: the hefty-lunged workhorse of the Tibetan Plateau. Among a life of grazing and hauling loads, these animals are utilised in every way. Their dense, dangling fur is used for coats. Their milk is drunk or turned into cheese and butter, their meat is consumed, and even their bones can be crafted into traditional horns. Despite these uses, I guessed why Yaks were named so, for it's the word you say each time you sniff the rancid beasts. Their scent is both akin to vomit and dust - *dusty vomit* - a smell which could squander the appetite of the most ravenous restaurant-goer.

On this occasion though, it was my finances which prevented my indulgence in a lavish local dinner. Foreign bank cards are not accepted in Tibetan areas, and so my pocket was reduced to the equivalent of seven pounds sterling. With my next destination another four hours away, I exercised frugality and munched on some cheap snacks for the evening.

I was eager for an early start. The droning dawn hum of Labrang Monastery could be heard nearby. The encircling monastery walls measure three kilometres and contain hundreds of barrel-sized prayer wheels. These wheels, when rotated, are believed to bring wisdom and purity while enhancing one's mind into a meditative state. Buddhists circumnavigate these long stretches of prayer wheels, spinning each one as they pass, to engage in a devout pilgrimage.

As the sun rose above the mountains, I followed the procession. Within the monastery wall, occasional chanting could be heard, along with the earthy pulsation of the Tibetan longhorn. There was something of this sound which resonated to my very bones. It rumbles like the land is groaning, and for all believers who hear it, it provides their call to prayer. I could imagine, as the horns echoed against the mountains, that the sound may have chilled the spine of approaching troops for centuries.

Some pilgrims sought further enlightenment by completing this circuit by doing prostrations; the previously described act of kneeling, lying flat on one's stomach with one's hands outstretched, then standing, taking three steps forward and repeating the process. One prostrating lady caught my attention. She was around ninety years old and her badly clouded eyes told me that she was blind. I watched her for a time as she performed these painful prostrations, her dust-covered nose twitching and her parched lips paining for water. At 3000 metres altitude, the air was thin here, and the cold remained harsh, yet she persevered.

Watching her made me think about the Chinese people in general. At some stage in China's history, turmoil has found each of its fifty-six ethnic groups, through war, oppression, torture, imprisonment or persecution. Yet the Chinese people, no matter their ethnicity, have mustered again and again against hardship. At first, for me, there seemed little splendour to behold in this vast and startling land, but now I realised that beauty was all around, and it existed in the hearts of the ordinary people. Now, against my expectations, I really didn't want to leave.

My time in this country was sadly coming to an end, yet a final challenge remained. 3000 kilometres of mountain and desert stood between myself and Kazakhstan, and I now had just four days left on my visa. After two nights in Xiahe, I caught an early bus to the Provincial capital of Lanzhou. Lying away from the Tibetan Plateau, this elongated city boasts some of the worst air quality in China. It was less breath-taking, and more breath-aching.

I continued into the city centre aboard a lunatic's scooter, who zoomed over a pedestrian footbridge, through a fruit and veg market and towards a disused railway line, where his gang of murderers were surely waiting for me. A few minutes later though, he dumped me on the roadside, twitched his neck, and scooted away.

I was left with the equivalent of eight pence in my pocket, and not the slightest clue where I would stay the night. For an hour I traipsed a busy street, testing countless ATMs without any luck and feeling hungry, having not eaten a good meal in days. Finally, Yuan in hand, I located a cool hostel on the top floor of a scruffy apartment block.

Here I met a young man named Liu who would serve as my Lanzhou guide. We spoke English together. It was liberating to hold a proper conversation with someone for the first time in a while, for without conversation one's mind only has itself to talk to, and one's mind can soon prove an unhealthy companion.

That evening, Liu insisted on taking me out for a dinner of

traditional Lanzhou noodles, which were delicious, before an unconventional dessert of chicken kebabs at a street-side shack.

'This is Uyghur food,' said Liu, 'from Xinjiang Province. Have you heard about it?'

'Xinjiang, yes, I will go there tomorrow.'

'*You're going to Xinjiang?*' Liu frowned.

'I have my ticket already; I will get the train from Lanzhou to Urumqi.'

'*Urumqi,*' Liu nodded in thought, 'you know, Oli, there are some problems in Xinjiang. You must be careful.'

'I only hope that I can get there.'

The next morning, with sixty hours to go, I made my first big mistake. I had booked a seat on a 13-hour high speed train to the city of Urumqi. Yet upon my arrival at the station in Lanzhou, the timetables showed no sign of my train. A ticket-seller confirmed what I had suspected, I was at the wrong station. My dash across Lanzhou during rush hour proved worthless. I had missed my train. Worse still, there were no available seats on any other trains to Urumqi for the rest of the day.

With limited options and time running out, I decided to puff up my chest, and try something audacious. Security at all Chinese transport hubs is at airport levels, and is heavily staffed with officers, but I reckoned if I could somehow sneak through, I might be able to slip onto another train bound for Urumqi.

'Bag,' said the officer, tapping the conveyor belt of the x-ray machine. I placed down my bag, and stepped through the body scanner. Nobody had asked for my ticket. I was through! I grabbed my bag and made towards the platform, but then, 'Sir!'

I calmly turned, and each of the five officers were looking at me.

'Bag on the table.'

I placed down my bag.

'Open it.'

I undid the zips and flicked through a couple of t-shirts to show there was nothing out of the ordinary inside my luggage. Yet something had snagged the scent of a stern female officer. She rummaged deeper into my bag and pulled out a bushcraft knife with a four-inch blade. She muttered something to the officer manning the x-ray screen, and returned to me.

'Anything else in your bag?'

'No, no,' I said, thinking about my two-foot long ice axe which could inflict untold damage in the wrong hands.

Mistrustful, the lady reached again into my bag and found my crampons (spiked metal plates which are fixed to mountain boots for climbing ice and snow, and which to the untrained eye probably look like medieval torture devices).

'Nothing else?' the officer returned.

'Nothing,' I lied once again, but she accepted my word.

'Follow me. Bring your bag.'

Feeling a complete idiot for getting myself into this mess, I followed the officer into a security office, where a pair of guards were lazing behind a desk. The officer handed over her bounty and pointed at me.

One guard, a chubby fellow with a serious face, rose from his chair and approached me. 'Passport.' I handed it to him. He flicked through, but showed little interest in it. 'Where are you going?'

'Urumqi.'

'Ticket.'

I passed him my ticket.

The guard bent it between his fingers and shook his head. 'Why are you going to Urumqi?'

'I'm going to Kazakhstan. I have only two days to get there.'

The guard paused, and returned my ticket and passport. 'Your train has gone. What are these?' he wrinkled his eyes at my crampons.

'Ah, for climbing mountains.'

'*For mountains*?'

'Yes! Can you help me?' I asked, 'I really need to get to Urumqi today. Please?'

For effect or through indifference, the guard scratched his head and pained over the decision, before slapping the back of his layabout colleague. 'Take him to the ticket office.' He turned back to me. 'I will keep the knife; you take these mountain things.'

I grumbled as I left him with my treasured six-year-old knife. The layabout was a voiceless young chap who deposited me before a smiling ticket lady. I explained my situation, and she trawled her computer.

'Ok, sir,' she said, after a time, 'I find one bed for you.'

'*Bed?*'

'Yes sir, for the 24-hour sleeper train.' She handed me the ticket. 'It leaves this afternoon.'

I'd always had a romantic notion of sleeper trains: of quaint wooden carriages gently chugging through the night, of the satisfying hoot of the steam-powered engine, of courteous conductors delivering the morning coffee, and perhaps of the faint lullaby of Victorian-era music from along the way.

Of course, this couldn't be further from the truth. Word spread that there was a backpacking westerner with a technicolour beard aboard. I shuffled down the narrow aisle beside the open cabins. A pair of excitable young boys began jumping on their beds and laughing when they saw me, which did little for my self-esteem.

I settled in an open cabin with a raucous family of five, the younger of whom were presently engaged in a pillow fight, and the older of whom (a lady in the bed above me) spent the first two hours dropping plum stones past my head and onto the floor. Every five minutes for the first four hours, the two excitable boys ran past me, laughed, pointed and waved, the novelty of which wore off immediately. Sanity came from the carriage beside us, where a group of students engaged in smart conversation. Less endearing was their constant flatulence.

Shortly, a sales trolley came trundling down the aisle, manned by the happiest woman I've ever seen. She was flogging all kinds of cheap electronic goods, and was especially ecstatic to present her items to me.

'Ah,' she said, pointing at me, then sticking her finger in the air, 'I know, I know.'

She began fumbling through her stock and I wondered which sensible item she thought best bestowed a gentleman of my standing: perhaps some high-tech solution for my daily needs, or a nice wristwatch, or a selection of brainteasing crosswords. The item she finally produced was a robotic neon fish, whom, when loaded with batteries, wiggled its head and tail and squirmed along the floor, while singing a preposterous and annoying tune which sounded suspiciously like a duck. The saleswoman beamed, and I thought long and hard about how I was portraying myself to other human beings.

'Erm, no thank you.' I replied.

This aquamarine cretin did catch the eyes of the two excitable boys through. And so, until the late hours of night, the entire carriage was overrun by the flashing, wriggling, quacking bastard, and a most abject hatred stewed in my mind for the designer, manufacturer, distributor and retailer of the godforsaken product.

At long last, Urumqi was in sight.

This city of three million is the provincial capital of Xinjiang Province, a region larger than any other in China, whose mountains and desert span from India to Mongolia. This is China's Central Asian frontier, and was at the heart of the ancient Silk Road. For modern day China, it is a highly sensitive region for both culture and geopolitics and in recent years has been the site of widespread conflict and unrest, mainly between the native Uyghurs and the Chinese state. An acrimony has festered here for half a century, and upon my exit from the train station in Urumqi, the tension remained palpable.

Dozens of soldiers guarded the forecourt outside the station, armed with assault rifles, wooden clubs, shields and gruesome-looking metal spears. Some stood in spiked cages, others clustered beside coils of barbed wire. Myself and the other passengers were directed through a tunnel of soldiers, two of whom requested my passport and gave me a brief questioning. It was an oppressing and deeply unwelcoming atmosphere. All happiness seemed sucked from the faces of the people by the guns of the watchful state.

As I continued into the city, more troops guarded each street corner, each offering me an observant eye. I avoided the soldiers when possible and instead found an alluring charm in the backstreets of Urumqi. Robed cooks sizzled chicken and lamb in exotic spices, street-side mosques throbbed with daytime devotees, and traders haggled over garments and grub. I was captivated at once, and this new world implied that Central Asia was nigh.

I eventually arrived at the International Bus Station, from where sleeper coaches radiate into the curious lands of Pakistan, Afghanistan, Tajikistan and Russia. My destination lay twenty-seven hours away and across a remote border post. I bought my ticket and a bagful of food. Then we aimed westward at dusk for the Kazakh frontier.

9

The sun lasted long on the horizon. It flashed orange between hundreds of grey apartment blocks, until it settled undisturbed upon the desert. Now, in late February, the sand was buried under a layer of indigo snow, whose windswept patterns stretched towards the edge of the earth. Temperatures of minus forty Celsius find these plains in the winter, while there are highs of forty in the summer. Night arrived early, then nought but infinite blackness remained outside my window. The bus crept on into the dark.

Inside, I was joined by a talkative bunch of Kazakh workers, journeying back to Almaty. Two potbellied men sat in their beds while sharing conversation and bottle of vodka across the aisle. A middle-aged husband and wife writhed their giant bodies in the narrow and uncomfortable beds. Meanwhile, the tough driver's mate, wearing a flat cap and leather jacket, became my watchman. He gave my shoulder a squeeze each time the bus stopped for a break. We would dash into the arctic cold and pee in the snow. Eventually, the bus grew quiet, and it pursued the rarely-travelled road deep into the night.

At ten the next morning, we eased our stiff bodies out onto a bus park. We were now just twenty miles from the border, and it appeared that I would reach Kazakhstan before my Chinese visa expired at midnight. As happens in these border areas, one is invariably mobbed by chancing money changers, each equipped with bulging piles of cash. Here, the exchange rate no longer fluctuates through changes in international financial markets, but through the devious whim of whomever is in possession of your so desired currency. I bargained a good price for a clutch of Kazakh Tenge and we soon continued to the border.

I realised that it was almost time to confess my sins. I had lied on my visa application, lied to the border guards, lied to every policeman who had stopped me in the street. I was not in China merely to tour the unrestricted Provinces of Yunnan and Sichuan. I had also stepped into the outskirts of Tibet and across secretive Xinjiang, but was that truly a crime? I arrived at the exit border not with some grand exposé on unseen China, nor was I the possessor of damning state secrets. China is one of the most ancient and ethnically diverse countries in the world, whose every cultural facet deserves to be witnessed and *celebrated*. My experience would have been diminished had I stuck to the tourist trail, as would my new-found love for China. I have long believed that there is nothing more stifling for one's life ambitions than comfort. This idea reigned true, for seeking discomfort in China had delivered untold splendour. For my sins then, I was guilty, yet unwilling to repent.

'Passport.' The potent word resounded.

I had been summoned by a slight female border officer with an attractive face. She took hold of my passport and offered me a fleeting glance. My reassuring smile went unnoticed. Five minutes elapsed. Once again, each page of my passport was scrutinised. Then, with only hours remaining on my visa, the decisive stamp descended, and no man's land beckoned. My month in China came to an end, and I departed with the hope that many future months here may ensue.

Getting into Kazakhstan was straightforward, with no visa required. However, I was unsettled as the final guard wished me 'Good luck!' when I ventured from the border post.

Ahead lay a fascinating leg of my expedition through the five countries which constitute *Central Asia*: Kazakhstan, Kyrgyzstan, Tajikistan, Uzbekistan and Turkmenistan. Borne from tribes and warlords, overwhelmed by Islamic crusaders, sacked by Genghis Khan, colonised by the Soviet Union, chopped into nations by Stalin and unexpectedly granted independence in 1991: to say that the region's history has been tumultuous is rather an understatement. The intervening generation has brought conflict, ethnic struggles, repression and dictatorships, but also liberalisation, smatterings of enormous riches, and whiffs of a democracy. Each nation represents a tapestry of tales in itself, through which I must navigate over the coming weeks. I knew not as I journeyed towards Almaty, that the road ahead would be more turbulent than any I have travelled before.

In a general sense, Kazakhstan has perhaps flourished more than its regional cousins, with vast oil wealth, a space program and a relatively tolerant regime. Almaty, the country's largest city, is also the cosmopolitan former capital. Indeed, it might be Amsterdam or downtown Paris to the groggy-eyed observer. And so it appeared to *me* as the sleeper bus finally reached the rain-swept city after my fifty hours of overland travel.

I found a simple guesthouse in the soviet-era suburbs, and was directed into a triple room. It was almost midnight, but I wanted to wander the city and loosen my creaking knees, yet the door into my room opened as I was about to leave.

'Oh, I have a neighbour.' A skinny man with weary eyes and a sharp nose entered. He was an Uzbek, and he introduced himself as Yoqub.

A curious phenomenon in this solo travelling game is that you never know who a person really is, or if what they are telling you is true, or what secrets may reside in their unspoken past. This may sound cynical, but when travelling you merely capture another human being for a fleeting moment of their existence. One relies on their self-portrayal and on one's own judgement to deem who it is that stands before you. Upon introduction, a brief mutual-reckoning ensues, and almost always, so does the exchange of trust. On this occasion though, the reckoning persisted longer than usual as I faced a most peculiar character. I could not pinpoint what, but there was something about Yoqub that was unsettling.

'Come here, my friend,' said Yoqub, 'you must join me for some food. It is Uzbek custom to share food with strangers.' He shifted from his bed, where he had some frugal possessions.

We sat together on a small table on edge of the room. Yoqub placed some cottage cheese and bread between us.

'What brings you to Almaty?' he asked.

'I've come here for the mountains. In a couple of days, when the weather clears, I'll travel south and try to reach a summit.'

'*Alone?*'

I nodded.

'You need to be careful, people have died in those mountains. You know that the Kyrgyz border lies across there too? Don't let the border guards see you there.'

'I'm always careful. Anyway, what are you doing in Almaty?'

'I'm working here.'

'What do you do?'

'Oh, I'm just in business.' Yoqub offered nothing more. 'Do you like the cheese? I eat it every night. I read that it's very good for your body. It makes you strong. I have stayed in this guesthouse for a while now, and I've met a few westerners. In the west, Islam gets a lot of bad press, so I always want to show westerners that sharing and kindness is very important in our religion.'

'Oh, I'm very aware of that,' I replied, 'I've spent time in the

Middle East -.'

'No, but the Middle East is different,' Yoqub snapped.
'There are many problems there, with terrorists and war. In
Uzbekistan, there are no such terrorists. Uzbekistan is the one place
where such bombings and killings could not happen. Back in 2005,
there was a small problem in the town of Andijan, but the Uzbek
government stopped this very quickly, and nothing has happened in
my country since then.'

The *incident* that Yoqub was referring to was a massacre in
May 2005 where government troops fired on unarmed protesters,
killing hundreds.

Yoqub proceeded to inform me about all the *western
stereotypes* he supposed I believed in, along with all the reasons his
country was great, before his line of conversation turned to religion.
His tedious rhetoric now became unpleasant as he asked about my
religious beliefs, of which mine are non-existent, before insulting me
for being foolish and attempting to show me the light of religion. I
told Yoqub that I had no interest in talking about the subject any
more, and that I was going to bed. Yet a bitterness had taken hold
which would remain for several days.

Heavy rains found Almaty for the next two days, meaning
that the nearby mountains were being buried under copious amounts
of snow. I figured that now would be a good time to readdress my
overall plan. My intention from the outset was to travel generally
south-west through Central Asia, following the mountains, before
looping through Iran and into Turkey. However, after several weeks
of frustrating emails and research, it seemed that this plan would not
be possible. Iran is a country which has fascinated me for many
years, and which seems to be adored by all tourists who have been
there. Presently, though, UK passport holders are only permitted in
the country if they are with a tour group or hire a private guide, the
costs of which were far above my budget.

Iran would have to wait. My reserve plan was to cross the
length of Turkmenistan, to a town named Turkmenbashi on the
Caspian Coast. From here, cargo ferries irregularly ply the sea
towards Baku, Azerbaijan, where I would pick up my route towards
Istanbul. I visited the Uzbek embassy to collect my visa for the
country, while making arrangements via email for my Azeri visa. I
had acquired my Tajik visa while in the UK, and all other countries
were easy to enter, except Turkmenistan, which I would tackle

nearer the time.

I escaped into the city when I could, visiting a mafia-style weaponry shop in some dubious backstreet to replace my confiscated knife, and sampling the hearty Kazakh cuisine at every chance. Meanwhile, spending longer than I wanted inside my room, I began to go a little stir-crazy. In lieu of any company, I began talking to myself more than could be considered normal. One day, I removed my clothes to see my full body in a mirror for the first time since entering Tibet. I looked surprisingly lean, if rather skinny. My hair and straggly beard were bleached blonde by the powerful mountain sun. Yet I felt fit. My rucksack no longer strained my shoulders, and my lungs were good and spacious. I still overdosed on painkillers to mask my knee pain each time I hit the trails, but I vowed to wean myself off. In all, when I looked in the mirror, I felt the rumble of an unbridled energy from within. Despite Yoqub's best efforts to bestow spiritual enlightenment, it was time for me to find solace in the mountains.

After two days of rain, only fog remained in Almaty. Laden with a fully-loaded expedition pack, I caught an early bus south on the advice of a local mountain guide. I was joined by a dozens of neon-clothed skiers, aiming for the Medeu Ski Resort on the promise of fresh powder. They were either Kazakhs or Russians, the latter of whom retain a large population here, and with whom I blended in nicely.

The Zailisky Alatau Range lay ahead: the towering northern boundary of the Tien Shan Mountains. This range is home to snow leopards, ex-soviet training bases and space observatories, yet nothing could be seen through the fog. I left the bus beside a narrow trail in the Medeu Valley at 1500 metres and began a long and undulating slog past farmhouses and into pine forest. I had reached a deserted winter wonderland, where all was white and silent. A shimmering hoar frost coated every needle upon the trees, and I swept through deep and fluid snow. Shortly and suddenly, all fog vanished from ahead. I pursued the trail onto a long plateau which overlooked the base of the valley.

The sky had been upturned, for the dense mist remained in the valleys, but above me and beyond the mountaintops, the sky was pristine blue. This was a rare temperature inversion, where warm, light air rises above a cold, dense weather system.

I could observe the Kazakh peaks for the first time. They rose from all directions like silver-summited contortionists: bent, crooked, leaning and lurching. Every slope was softened by several feet of untouched snow – dumped by the recent storm - and the trail ahead was blank. As I continued below the midday sun, I trudged along short, exact bearings, trying to keep to a hardened path below the knee-deep snow. One step in the wrong direction would leave me down to my stomach in powder. I crossed a faintly running stream and began to ascend a steep 900 metre slope. The climbing was hard and sustained, as I wove through occasional pine trees, and over corniced snow. A final climb across a sheer ice sheet brought me to a high ridge; one side of which was a gradual slope, the other, a precipitous cliff.

After nine hours, I reached my first summit: Kumbel (3200m). It was six o'clock and night was coming, so I dug a snow-trench beside a boulder, gorged on rations and settled into my bivi bag. A greater objective awaited tomorrow.

As the sun descended on mountain paradise, the sky became my cinema. Blue became orange, and orange turned black. As all traces of light vanished, stars began to appear. The milky way glistened indigo and gold, then shooting stars flashed across the celestial sphere. It was minus ten where I lay, yet the cold could not penetrate my thick sleeping bag. So I rested, enamoured by the infinite cosmos, until a happy thought struck my mind.

I retrieved my phone and saw that I had full signal. I called Emma. The phone continued to ring until I reached the voicemail. All I wanted was to hear Emma's voice, yet the silence beyond the beep allowed me to pull words from my mind as if in a daydream, and like so I spoke. I told Emma of where I lay, and of the scene before my eyes in all its glorious colour, and that I was smiling as I spoke and was immensely content, but also that I missed her deeply and that I wished more than anything that she was lying next to me now.

'I love you,' I said, before I ended the call.

The moon shortly set the mountains and sky aglow and the starlight spectacle ebbed away. Then, I found a deep and soothing sleep and did not wake until dawn.

My aim for the day was to continue along the ridgeline to the distant summit of *Titova* (3800m), then make a steep descent down to Medeu. Between myself and Titova lay a number of scrambles over smaller peaks, along with a bare snow slope.

There lies in mountaineering an eternal paradox between danger and fear, whereby a climber on a vertical cliff may be afraid, yet in little actual danger given the strength of his ropes and karabiners. Conversely, an alpinist on a snow-covered mountainside in pristine conditions will have no fear whatsoever, but may well be exposing themselves to lethal danger in the form of an unseen avalanche.

Like so, through the sun, the wondrous landscape and the shooting stars, I had fallen into a mistaken sense of security, yet I was wandering alone into danger. Overnight, I had filled my water bottles with snow and kept them by my feet in my sleeping bag. Such were the temperatures though, that I had little water come morning, and I was without a stove. Becoming dehydrated, I stopped among a patch of brush, built a small fire and melted snow in an old sweetcorn tin. It tasted awful.

The mountains remained silent today. Clouds still lingered in the valleys, and the hot sun shone from above. I reached the snow slope at late-morning, later than was ideal. By now the slope had been basking in the sun for several hours. Yet this slope, rising for three hundred metres, provided the only route towards Totiva. It glistened over me, a hulking untouched tower of snow, the top of which could not be seen as it bent away in the distance. It appeared like a giant airship that had landed on the mountain and been covered by the blizzard.

I began to climb, and felt that the snow was deep and loose. I wanted to tread quickly and lightly, but the terrain was taxing. Aiming directly uphill, I began to near the top of this mound. Then, in immediate succession, two paralysing things occurred.

First, a colossal bang resounded across the peaks. I watched as a huge corniced edge tumbled down a cliff beside the snow slope. It rumbled out of sight for what felt an eternity. Then, I looked down to find with great alarm that a giant crack had broken in the snow beneath me, stretching for several metres on either side.

Paralysed I remained, unwilling to go on, yet uncertain to go back.

10

Whichever way I turned, forwards or backwards, I knew that an eight-hour trek loomed. I had climbed into a remote corner of Kazakhstan's mountains and there was not a soul in sight. I had not moved a millimetre since my eyes fell on the expanding crack beside my feet. The slope was prone. Urgency was required but decision was faltering. Commit to the slope and ascend, or retreat with haste?

The sun sizzled on my neck. I tasted my parched lips and took a chancing breath. Then, on the promise of a familiar route, I rotated and charged down the hill. What the hell was I doing? Mountains are no playground. I should have woken in the early hours of morning and climbed while the snow was hard. But my logic faltered as my mind was mesmerised by the nightscape. What a fool I had been.

Decision made though, it was time to get out of here. I escaped the slope, and ran clear of any avalanche path. Yet my troubles were not over. I was already out of water again, and my dehydration left me feeling dizzied. I trekked back along the ridgeline, counting Kumbel as my Kazakh peak, before reaching the ice sheet above the main descent. After ten paces downhill, my crampon twisted on a hidden rock. I was caught in a lapse of concentration. My body twisted. I fell and began to slide down the ice sheet. My ice axe flew out of my hand, and slid downhill ahead of me. Without my axe, I had no way of stopping. I couldn't dig my fingers into the solid ice. In a moment of sheer serendipity, my ice axe clinked against a protruding rock. I grabbed it as I slid past and managed to perform an ice axe arrest to save me from sliding off the mountain. Perhaps, after all, Yoqub was right. Maybe there is a God.

I cursed myself once again, and followed my footprints down a 900 metre snow slope to a stream, where I hacked through ice and devoured crystalline water. Having walked for twelve hours, I finally reached the roadside after nightfall. Within seconds I managed to flag down a passing car and hitch a ride back into the city. Half an hour later I was gobbling a burger in Almaty; filthy and wild-haired among the watching diners.

Today had provided a warning shot. High mountains could be known, in a euphemistic way, as mortality consultants. For there comes a time when one realises how imperious and everlasting the mountains are - the wise watchmen of the world – and how fragile and temporary one's own existence is in comparison. A rock fall could so easily bludgeon my brittle skull and splatter my brains across the ground. An avalanche could sweep my flimsy body down the mountainside and crush me beneath tons of concrete ice. The freezing cold could bite into my extremities, and gradually envelop my body in a comatose state, from which I would never wake. Here in the highlands, the Grim Reaper prowls. No years of experience or planning or training can allow a man to fully defy the whim of the mountain.

Who was I to face these monsters? I do not proclaim to be an expert mountaineer, and my years are still young. Each time I present myself alone to the mountains, I also submit to them. I could splay my arms and declare, 'You are my master, have mercy on me.'

My respect for the mountains was growing with every climb of my expedition, as was my fear, as was my love. They may bring adrenaline or accident, ecstasy or death. One moment the mountains are paradise, the next they could be hell.

Among these thoughts was Emma and my family, who at home shared none of my rapture, but all of my worry and more. With them in mind, perhaps the mountains today had cautioned me on purpose: '*Tread with care, young man, or you will tread no more.*'

Fortunately, Yoqub wasn't there when I got back to the guesthouse. I was asleep before he returned, and I left the next morning before he rose.

I was making the short journey into Kyrgyzstan, and the rugged heartland of Central Asia. This is one of the most mountainous countries on the planet, with an average elevation of almost 3000 metres. It is a far poorer country than Kazakhstan, bearing no significant oil or gas reserves. Yet I understood that this jagged republic is home to some of the hardiest and most ancient mountain communities on the planet.

The Kyrgyz national identity largely spawns from Manas: a legendary horse-bound hero. It is told that one thousand years ago, a child was born with rare qualities of bravery, charisma and strength. A master of both horses and men, he gathered together and led Kyrgyzstan's forty clans to fight off the attempted invasions of the Uyghurs and Afghans. The epic tales of Manas are recited today in traditional gatherings by expert storytellers, who use music and singing to portray Manas' intrepid battles.

In my mind, as I crossed the Kyrgyz border, the country which lay ahead promised everything I sought to find on this expedition. When I arrived in the capital though, my first conversation enlightened me on the dark modern-day menace which is sweeping the country.

Bishkek is an unglamorous city compared to Almaty. There is a general greyness to the square and simple streets, but the city is not unwelcoming. Here and there, busy green spaces could be found, along with the kind of austere statues and squares that one might expect to see in an ex-soviet capital. Families enjoyed a ramshackle amusement park, and there was an obvious sense of community spirit, as groups of youths swept leaves outside their concrete apartment blocks. Bishkek was a curious and unpretentious place, which I somehow liked at once.

It was in my hostel by the city where I met a man named Meder. He was lazing on his bed with a can of lager. He had a pot-belly, gold teeth (like many Kyrgyz), and scars on his face. He was evidently a tough man, who offered the firmest handshake. With a swig of beer, he opened conversation with a question one could never pre-empt.

'What are the prisons like in your country?'

'I'm not sure,' I frowned. 'They are ok, I think.'

'They are easy?'

'I think so.'

Meder scowled, before breaking into a drunken laugh. 'The prisons in Kyrgyzstan are hard. Here in Central Asia, we have the worst prisons in the world.'

Knowing that this gentleman would soon be sleeping just several feet away from me, I hoped that his enthusiasm for the subject of incarceration was either derived from watching documentaries, or from serving as an honourable prison guard.

'They are disgusting,' he returned. 'There are dozens of men in every cell, and you sleep on the floor. If you need a shit, you just shit in the corner. And if you are gay – you know, gay? – they will make you eat the shit. Every cell, it has a boss, and if you do something wrong and make the boss angry, then the boss and his gang will stab you, or kill you. But if you have money,' his teeth gleamed, 'you can live like a king. The prisons are the same in Tajikistan and Uzbekistan. People are like rats in there. Have you ever been to prison?'

'Erm, no.'

'Do not go to prison in Kyrgyzstan.'

'What would happen if I did?'

Meder looked up at me with a smirk, which became a full-blown belly laugh which sent tears to his eyes, 'They will kill you!'

I found myself laughing too, for I expected to hear nothing less.

Meder eventually mellowed, and spoke with a deeper voice. 'I am here in Bishkek on business.' He had a small briefcase, some more cans of beer, and nothing else.

'I see, and what do you?'

'Selling,' Meder leant closer, '*selling drugs.*'

Since the collapse of the Soviet Union - when Central Asia became five separate nations - poverty, corruption and unguarded border zones have provided a hotbed for heroin trafficking. From the opium-growing heartlands of Afghanistan, the drug travels northwards through the region and towards the strangled veins of Russian and European addicts. It's estimated that twenty-five percent of all the world's heroin passes through Kyrgyzstan, the vast majority of which slips past bribed or unsuspecting officers. In turn, illicit wealth finds crime kingpins or high-level officials, and tantalising bounties await for small-time 'salesmen' like Meder.

The next morning, I thanked Meder for the pleasure of his acquaintance, and hoped that I may never see him again. Still intoxicated by Kazakhstan's highland utopia, and with heavy snow forecast in a couple of days' time, I aimed for the mountains once more. One-hour south of Bishkek lies the Ala-Too range; a jagged array of accessible peaks, which were presently deserted for the winter months. A taxi was my only means of accessing the lonesome trailhead, *Alplager*, which sits at 2100 metres.

From here, paths wind across valleys and glaciers towards dozens of summits, many of which represent technical climbs. My target was Komsomolets Peak (4150m); a mountain which I knew almost nothing about, but which, according to the contours on my GPS, seemed doable alone, depending on conditions.

On the morning of my arrival there, the skies were melancholy. They turned the landscape a brooding shade, and from my first steps forward, I felt the distinct sense of isolation. After walking-in along the valley, my climb began with a 1500 metre ascent up a scree and snow slope to a high ridge. From there, the ridge extended for several kilometres towards Komsomolets. The snow was often sparse on this south-facing ridge, but it accumulated more as I ascended. Overhead, for twenty minutes, I was pursued by magnificent eagle, circling above and perhaps wondering whether I was an edible morsel.

As night drew close, I set my bivouac on the ridgeline at 4000 metres, and this was when my true challenge began. Twilight arrived quickly among oncoming clouds. They mustered overhead, and the temperature began to plummet. I lay in my sleeping bag, having snacked on bread and cheese, ready to wait out the night. The temperature gauge on my watch told me it was minus ten, then minus fifteen. Snow began to fall at midnight, and a wicked wind swirled from the south.

I wore everything I owned, and was huddled inside my sleeping bag and bivouac. The weather front had arrived a day early, and there was nothing I could do. Wind chill made the temperature around minus thirty, and an intense stinging pain was spreading through my feet. I was truly on the edge of warmth; my kit was good, but it was not built to withstand such temperatures. Shards of snow skipped across my uncovered face, and the minutes dragged by. I managed only an hour or two of sleep. Beside me, my camera, food and walking boots had all frozen solid. I used my bag as an improvised windbreak, but it didn't reduce the cold. As dawn approached, and the faintest glimmer of daylight awoke the darkened sky, I could see that the weather was set to worsen still.

This was one of those distinct moments where I had to ask myself '*how much do I want it?*' Do I get out of my sleeping bag and step into the blizzard? Do I lace my frozen boots onto my freezing feet? Do I pack my things and throw my heavy rucksack onto my shoulders? Do I journey on step after step, despite the altitude, and the cold and the hunger, cross a perilous ridge, just to satisfy my inconsequential aim of summiting a still distant mountain? It was an aim which mattered to no other person in the world but me.

It was then, as I lay among the snowstorm at six in the morning, that a powerful thought struck my mind; a thought which has stayed with me since that day. I realised that everything I thought was stopping me from reaching the summit – the cold, the blizzard, the altitude and the hunger - didn't really matter. The only real barrier between myself and the summit, *was me*. I knew I had the skills I needed to go on, but did I have the guts, the drive, the resilience?

With a surge of inspiration, I climbed out of my sleeping bag, laced up my frozen boots (running on the spot for ten minutes to ease the pain in my feet), shouldered my expedition pack, and advanced into the blizzard. It was a lonesome slog to the craggy summit, but upon my arrival I was overwhelmed by a delirious euphoria and I yelled into the blizzard. Freedom, solitude, adrenaline and fear circled in my mind. This is why I quit my day job, and this is why, despite their danger, the mountains always lure me back. Life on the edge, I thought, or life over!

Abreast a wave of surging energy, I raced downhill, skidding through snow and scree, to arrive in the marginally warmer climes of Alplager, just four hours later. With no reason to linger as the snow persisted, and my food dwindled, I filled my lungs and set towards Bishkek. Unfortunately, it was forty kilometres away. There were a few cars around, but no people. After half an hour of walking though, I managed to hitch a ride with a kind local family. They fed me chocolates and drove me directly to my hostel without accepting a penny.

When I told them about camping on the mountain ridge, the mother gasped, 'Weren't you worried about eagles pecking your face?'

'No,' I replied, 'but I guess I should have been!'

Foreign tourists are very sparse in Central Asia, especially during the winter. Indeed, I had not encountered a Western traveller since meeting Emma in Chengdu. It was refreshing the next evening to find a small bar in the centre of the city, frequented by a cluster of fascinating people.

I fell in with two Kyrgyz ladies, two US Marines, an American traveller and an Afghan charity worker. Our conversation was immediately deep, topical and interesting, stimulating my mind and my long-rested vocal chords. We won a pub quiz in the bar, before the local brew plied its heady course into my bloodstream. As we traipsed the taverns of Bishkek into the early hours, my inebriation mingled with my mountain-borne adrenaline. I found an intense hedonistic state. Music, dancing and booze edged me deeper into my sense of freedom. That night, my place on earth felt divine. I was unemployed, untethered, unconcerned; liberated to the Nth degree, until a haze smeared my euphoria and put an end to all recollection.

11

I awoke on the floor of a dreary Soviet-era apartment in the outskirts of Bishkek. It was early, but all my friends had already left. Slapping my forehead, and downing a glass of water, I emerged in a rainy communal garden. The garden was unkempt, with weeds stooping in the drizzle. Rusting Ladas lined the potholed street between the encircling apartment blocks. Nobody was around, but a couple of forlorn faces looked down at me from the surrounding windows.

This place was as stark and ordinary as could be. I had expected Kyrgyzstan to reveal itself differently than it had done so far. Had the nomadic legions of Manas evaporated into history? What of the storytellers, the horsemen, the wrestlers, the costumes and the colour? Out of the backstreets, the main road plied a direct route through the suburbs. I passed the vandalised outer wall of a desolate prison. Two guards, chins nuzzled in their collars, watched me as I passed. A disused rail track split the road in two, aiming through lifeless wildflowers to a wooden barricade beyond.

Rain interspersed mist and smog, and the few figures who wandered the streets appeared like shadows before the grey. I was walking through an LS Lowry painting.

Utterly drenched, I reached my hostel an hour later, and gave a stiff knock on the locked front door.

Elina, the hostel owner, opened the door. 'Mr France! I thought you had gone missing!' She hurried me inside.

'I'm sorry, Elina, I was partying last night, and…'

Elina smiled and shook her head. 'Come and get some porridge.'

I followed her into the kitchen. Elina ladled a portion of steaming oats from the saucepan into a bowl, and sat opposite me while I ate.

I took a mouthful, and then started, 'I think I need to leave the city. It's no good for me. I want to explore the *real* Kyrgyzstan, the people of the mountains.'

'That's not so easy now.'

I frowned.

'Most of those villages are cut-off in the winter time, and sometimes they are abandoned until the snow melts.'

'I've read about a village in the south – *Arslanbob* – do you know it?'

A vision found Elina's mind. She looked into the air as though into her memory. '*Arslanbob*. I went there every summer as a child. There are walnut groves across the mountainside, and waterfalls and forests, and so many flowers. It is a beautiful village, Mr France, but what you will find there in the winter time, I do not know.'

'Is it possible to get there?'

Elina tipped her head, 'You can try, but it's a very long drive. You must go to the Bazaar early in the morning. Aim for the shared taxis and ask for Arslanbob. Good luck.'

As I thanked Elina for the porridge, a Malaysian man entered, introducing himself as Sam. He was an expressive and energetic man.

'Another foreigner!' he proclaimed.

I nodded, 'Nice to meet you, sit down if you like.'

Sam took Elina's vacated seat. We spoke for a while as Sam grimaced through his bowl of porridge, '*Do you actually like this food?*'

Elina glanced over.

'I could eat it every day!'

Sam pushed away his bowl, his face contorting as he swallowed the final mouthful.

'Ah,' he sat back, 'but I am happy to be in Bishkek; it is much better for doing business here. I have just returned from Dushanbe [capital of Tajikistan], and I had many problems. You must be careful if you go!' Sam wagged his finger.

'What happened?'

'The police,' Sam tutted and shook his head. 'I was walking to my hostel late at night. Three police officers stopped me on the street. They told me, 'Show us your passport!' So I showed them, and asked, 'Is there a problem?' The policemen nodded, 'Problem.' They led me into their car and drove away onto a quiet street. 'Empty your pockets, empty your pockets!' they told me. I showed them my wallet and my phone and said 'I have nothing.' The policeman sitting next to me – a very fat man – took my wallet and opened it. He took out fifty dollars and said, 'For me, ok?' but I replied, 'No! No! I've done nothing wrong.' The policemen looked at each other, then the fat one pointed his gun at me, 'Fifty dollars, for me. Ok?' *I can't believe what is happening!* 'I am a businessman!' I told them. The fat man pushed his gun against me, and then I gave up. I say, 'Ok, ok, ok. Take the money, take the money.' So they return my passport and let me out the car.'

Elina, who had been listening with a curious ear, turned and left the kitchen. Then Sam leant forwards. 'You need to be careful in Central Asia. It is not like your country. You can't always trust the officials. Actually, you need to avoid them sometimes. Just remember that.'

The rains endured throughout the day. It was so gloomy and dampening – of both the streets and one's spirits – that I remained in the hostel until dusk. I had been invited that evening to re-join my friends for a traditional home-cooked meal. We gathered in the dreary apartment by the garden.

Aziza and Aya, our Kyrgyz hosts, were busy in the kitchen cooking a regionally famous rice and meat dish called *plov*. Meanwhile, Dan, the lively American traveller, was telling the rest of the group about one of Kyrgyzstan's stranger traditions.

'Hey, come listen to dis, Aali,' said Jake, a colossal US marine working at the American embassy.

'So, Oli,' said Dan, flashing his eyes, 'here in Kyrgyzstan, a man will choose a woman. Then, he follows her, waiting for his chance. When she's alone, completely alone, the man forces her into his car and drives away, stealing her from her family.'

'What are you talking about? To take her hostage?'

'Naw, man, naw!' said Jake.

'So,' said Dan, 'Once the man has got the woman under control, he will call her family and make his demand: *I want to marry your daughter.*' It's called bride kidnapping. It's illegal now, but apparently it still happens all the time.'

Aya came into the room. Jake turned 'Aya, what would you do if someone tried to kidnap you?'

Aya shrugged and smiled, 'It depends.'

'Whatchu mean?'

'Sometimes, if the man and the woman love each other, they organise the kidnapping together. Then, there is no need to negotiate a price for the bride, and no need for an expensive wedding. But if it was a stranger, or someone like you, Jake, there is no way I would marry him.'

Jake chuckled, 'Aww man!'

Later that evening, I smoked a traditional hookah pipe with

the group. This glorified bong is an Asian institution; a centrepiece for wise conversation and debate for centuries. Its burning tobacco sweeps down a glass tube, bubbles through water, and floods into the heaving lungs of its handler, providing a lightness of mind. In a moment of near diplomatic crisis and cultural insult though, the narrating smoker experienced such an acute lightness of mind that he almost tumbled backwards off his seat. I pardoned myself from the group, floated to the bathroom and reacquainted my purging throat with Aziza's plov. This city may well have been my downfall had I not managed to escape.

Despite the invitation to another party the following night, I opted to travel to the fabled land of walnuts and waterfalls: *Arslanbob.*

The conventional mode of transport in this region is the shared taxi, a car or minibus which is used by a collection of strangers. It leaves when full and its price is as keen as one's bartering skills. I arrived at the central bazaar early in the morning. To the imaginative eye, this might be ancient Persia. Dusty traders ply the ramshackle marketplace. Their wit is sharp and their tongue is fast: haggling, quibbling, jostling, touting. These bazaars are a lion's den for the uninitiated.

The shared taxi rank is always obvious, for it lies beside the ubiquitous gang of *flat-caps.* The flat-caps, as I named them, are the cluster of portly taxi drivers who like to wear dark jackets, dark trousers, dark boots, gold teeth and flat-caps. They huddle together in intimidating swarms, sometimes arguing, sometimes playing cards, sometimes laughing, but always fuelled by laddish testosterone. At least one of the flat-caps stays on the lookout for customers; customers typically being tough Kyrgyz women with a stiff-arm like a prop-forward. The flat-cap's greatest prize, though, is the journeying foreigner.

'Issyk-kol? Karakol? Osh?' A watching flat-cap saw me coming.

'No,' I shook my head, 'Arslanbob.'

'Arslanbob! Arslanbob!'

The word spread through the flat-cap swarms. Ears pricked up. Eyes came alight.

'Arslanbob! Arslanbob!'

I was quickly surrounded by twenty men, through whom an old flat-cap was shoved towards me.

'Arslanbob,' the crowd shouted, pointing at the old flat-cap.

We met in the centre of the group and engaged in a momentary stand-off. His face was pitted and scared and each of his remaining teeth glistened gold. He was short and squat, and displayed an ugly set of tattoos on his forearms.

The crowd quietened, urging me to confront the old flat-cap. To his advantage: wisdom and practice. To mine: only faltering ingenuity.

He bowed his head at me. '*Arslanbob?*'

I bowed at him. '*Yes.*'

Then, adhering to convention, our palms met in a bracing handshake.

The old flat-cap began, 'Three thousand Som.' He squeezed my hand.

I flicked my head, 'One thousand.'

'Ah-haha-haha.' The crowd laughed and jeered.

My adversary returned with a smirk. 'Two-and-half-thousand.' His grip became tighter.

I offered a courteous nod, but held my ground, 'One-thousand.'

The crowd grumbled and chattered. I was up for the fight.

Our hands were locked. Our gaze was set.

'Two-thousand,' said the flat-cap.

'One-thousand, two-hundred.'

He gave a deep inhale, and shook his head, '*One-and-half-thousand.*'

I held his gaze a moment more, then nodded, 'One-and-a-half-thousand.'

We shared a final handshake. Then, deal-done, the crowd dispersed and I followed the old flat-cap to his waiting car. He introduced himself as Almaz. His English was rudimentary, but he knew how to barter. I settled in the rear of his seven-seater, and was joined over the next thirty minutes by a large family of two men, two women, one grandmother, four children, and a crying baby. After pausing at their suburban apartment, to load the car beyond bursting point, we were on our way.

I was settled beside a well-dressed man, and his child. The man had neatly combed hair and a clean-shaven face, and he spoke good English. He shared a home cooked meal with me, and we soon started talking.

'I work for the Kyrgyz drug enforcement agency. In recent years, the drug problem here in Kyrgyzstan has been getting worse. More drugs than ever are coming through the country, but it's much harder for us to stop the flow.'

'But why is it more difficult?'

'Because so many people are involved. The criminal networks used to be small and more easy to track. Five years ago, we stopped a car and found fifty kilos of heroin. *Fifty kilos!* Now, with Kyrgyzstan being a poor country, many people are getting involved in moving and selling drugs. *Everybody wants to earn some drug money.* We do not have the people to track and stop everybody, so the drugs are slipping past us more easily. But we know that *the drugs are right under our noses.*'

After cruising out of Bishkek, we began the long ascent of a high mountain pass which rises above 3500 metres. Often cut-off in the winter, a herd of bulldozers had been working the snowdrifts to ensure we could continue. A thick fog obscured any mountain views. Our only sight was the occasional rundown building on the roadside.

Almaz was a painfully slow driver, and his overloaded car struggled along the undulating roads. Myself and the other passengers passed between conversation and slumber as the hours dwindled by. We crept over a second pass above 3000 metres before descending to the large Toktogul reservoir. Here we stopped at a café at nightfall. While we ate, Almaz watched from inside his car as he made some phone calls.

By 10pm, as heavy rains began to fall, we reached the small industrial town of Toshkomur. Almaz navigated through a dark neighbourhood and parked outside a metal gate. Here, the family disembarked, leaving me alone with Almaz to continue towards Arslanbob. But something didn't seem right. Instead of returning to the main road, Almaz crept along some deserted backstreets until he noticed the dipped headlights of a parked car across the road. My guard was up, my senses heightened. Why was Almaz bringing me here?

Easing to a halt, Almaz looked at me, but didn't say a word. He stared at the car across the way, until his phone began to ring.

Almaz answered. 'Da [Yes].'

He reached across me and took a small package out of the glovebox. Gesturing for me to stay, Almaz climbed out into the rain as a hooded figure approached. They each looked at me, and I held their gaze. Then, Almaz handed the figure a package, and received 4000 Kyrgyz Som (£45) in return.

Retreating into the car, my criminal cabbie revealed his golden teeth. The drug agent's nose was closer to his prize than he may have suspected.

We continued at a snail's pace, as Almaz became increasingly tired and grumpy. He swigged from a hip flask and leant over his steering wheel to peer through the rain and fog; his cloudy eyes heavy and strained. Sometimes he barked at me to remind him where we were going. The unlit roads meanwhile were awash with hazards: speeding lorries, deep potholes, unmarked bends and roadside cliffs.

I urged myself to stay awake, mainly to keep Almaz from falling asleep. We ought to have stopped, but with villages sparse and desolate in the dead of night, where could we go? Finally, at 2.30am we arrived in the disappointingly ugly centre of Arslanbob, at 1700 metres. Almaz gestured a question asking where I would spend the night. All I had was the phone number of the only home-stay in town. Almaz called, but there was no answer. The skies thundered with rain, and I had no clue where I would stay. Perhaps I could find shelter in the central market.

I had learned already that Almaz could be an irritable and unpleasant man, not to mention the fact that he was a drug dealer, but I sensed that he wanted to help me. He left the car and started banging on the metal gates of several houses. Barking dogs erupted, but no people showed.

Almaz returned and raised his hands. Tiredness had consumed us both. He lay flat the rear seats, and I reclined in the front. Wrapped in blankets, Almaz quickly fell asleep. I, meanwhile, shivered until dawn amid the chorus of the snoring, flatulent, opium-peddling pensioner who had brought me here. How I missed my beautiful fiancée.

The morning sun did not find Arslanbob the next day, rather, a ghostly brightness radiated through the pervasive downpour. Almaz called the home-stay once more, and with luck, they answered, sending a car into the village to collect me some minutes later. Almaz and I shared a warm handshake before parting for pastures new.

I arrived at a farmyard outside the village, where a conservatively dressed young lady showed me to a simple room. The family woke me three hours later, bearing a tray of dumplings, bread, jam and tea.

'We don't have many visitors at this time of year,' the young lady told me, 'but there is a Frenchman staying in the room next door. Perhaps you would like to meet him.'

It seemed the Frenchman was still asleep for now, so I opened my window and gazed outside while I sipped on tea. Arslanbob is home to the largest walnut grove on earth, whose wide varieties are said to have been the origin for walnut plantations around the world. According to legend, the Prophet Mohammad entrusted an honest man with finding paradise. The man arrived in this beautiful valley with mountains and waterfalls, but devoid of trees. So the Prophet gave the man a bag of seeds, which the man scattered from the nearby mountaintop to create Arslanbob's Garden of Eden.

I regretted the rain, and the dense, bulbous clouds which reached into the atmosphere, and the drifting fog which travelled as sweeping shadows. Paradise was tarnished by a gloomy veil which showed no signs of dissipating.

I shortly convened with the waking Frenchman, and we enjoyed a good moan about the weather, before venturing into the village. Arslanbob was an ethnic Uzbek community. Its residents were dressed modestly: the women in headdresses and skirts, and the old men with long, silver beards and skullcaps. Like the flat-caps, these elderly men gathered in small groups around the village square, chattering and watching us as we went by. It was a quiet place where I figured that nothing of any great circumstance ever occurred. Residents tended their treasured patches of land, traders sold food in the market, and the years drifted uneventfully by. Had I wandered here on a bright September day, when the villagers were harvesting walnuts and traditional games were being played, I am sure my impression of the village would have been different. Today though, everything seemed inconsequential.

Having seen the walnut groves beside the mountain streams, the Frenchman and I decided to leave Arslanbob; him for the north, me for the south. Tajikistan lay ahead, but my arduous journey towards its capital was only just beginning.

12

I needed a calling. I always knew that Central Asia was a mountain climbing playground, and to this end the region had excelled. But I wanted more. I sought a place to take me into the human heart of these rugged lands: a town, a village, a community, a place of magic and intrigue. A place to live long in my memory. It may have been Arslanbob, were it not for the drizzling dullness and Almaz the dope-dealer. I felt certain that such a place must exist, but I did not know where. Who would summon me then, like the old Monk in Laos who cast his finger to an unknown mountain, or the nomad by the Tibetan stove who guided me towards Langmusi? As I continued southwards through the region, I whetted my senses, ready to be summoned.

A five-hour journey delivered me to one of the most ancient cities in Central Asia. Osh is a sprawling place and is home to the largest bazaar in the entire region, where once silks and other fineries were traded, and where now almost anything can be purchased, from satsumas to songbirds, tunics to traditional hats, goldfish to gold rings. It stretches for a kilometre towards the city's central spire: the rocky outcrop of Sulayman-Too, the supposed burial place of the prophet, Solomon. This marks the midpoint of the ancient Silk Road, and, approximately too, the midpoint of my journey across Asia.

I spent two days exploring Osh, meeting, among many people, a very curious shopkeeper. He was a young man, who wore a baggy white hoody which probably belonged to his dad, and some large headphones around his neck. 'Hey, are you from England?' He asked, when I placed my water on the counter.

'Yes I am.'

'Oh my God!' His face went red. 'I love England! I can't believe this. My name's Erik.'

I raised my eyebrows, savouring the moment of raised status. 'Yes I've lived in England all my life. I'm from a town called Wigan. You may have heard of it.'

He smiled and frowned at the same time.

'It's in the north, near, erm, Manchester.'

'Ohhh, *Manchester*, that's so amazing.'

'So, what makes you love England?' *The classic, green*

countryside, I wondered, *the quintessential sights of London, or did he just love a good plate of fish and chips?*

'Ah, man, I love the rap music!'

'*Rap music?*'

'Yeah, rap music. My favourite rapper is Plan B. I can teach you one of his songs if you like?'

'Erm.'

'Wait, wait, you just beat on the counter, like this.' Erik, began drumming his hands: *dum-ch, du-du-dum-dum-ch, dum-ch, du-du-dum-dum-ch.*

I took over: *dum-ch, du-du-dum-dum-ch.*

Then Erik started rapping.

I kept the beat going, louder and louder, swinging my head like a manic giraffe, and turning Erik's shop into a boom box. I was getting gripped by the rhythm. Erik's words were divine. My beat was hot. We would tour the world!

'Wait,' said Erik.

An old lady entered, purchased a dozen eggs, some bread and a small block of cheese. She flicked through a handful of change, and deposited some on the counter. She looked at Erik, then she looked at me. Then she left, and the beat returned.

Dum-ch, du-du-dum-dum-ch.

We could take Kyrgyzstan by storm, then work on breaking America. Our band name: *Oli and the Anglophile.* Erik finished his rap and I rounded off the beat by symbol-smashing a pile of coins. We fist-bumped and I've never felt so cool in my life.

'That was awesome!' said Erik.

'Yeah,' I breathed, 'pretty awesome.'

Erik and I vowed to reunite in England sometime, during Erik's quest to distribute his mixtape. Until then, I had a quest of my own. Tajikistan awaited the following day.

I hitched a ride towards the border with a travelling salesman. I enjoyed a thirty-minute phone-conversation with his English-speaking wife. This somehow turned into a strange marital therapy session as the lady complained about her husband's many failures. After voicing my thoughts, she concluded that she would send him to Russia.

The salesman dropped me in the border town, Batken, by mid-morning. I bade him goodbye, and hoped that his future in Moscow would be prosperous.

The nearby border post is a notorious drug smugglers route, yet, travelling by bus, the crossing felt remarkably relaxed. The Tajik border guards were dutiful but friendly. They did make one mistake though, forgetting to give me a vital immigration card. I hoped that their blunder would not cause me any repercussions.

My first impression of Tajikistan was that the country seemed wealthier than its Kyrgyz neighbour, although the nation is actually poorer per capita. Its roads and buildings were in good condition, and there was a smattering of gold and Tajik flags in the centre of every community. I enjoyed clear skies for the first time in days, and the sun set alight, at almost every turn, the permeating portrait of an unfamiliar man. This man had a round face, thick black eyebrows and a neat, square haircut.

I watched from the bus window as a series of giant billboards relayed the abstract adventures of this mysterious chap. Sometimes he wandered through a superimposed mountain pasture, or shook hands with a group of poor farmers, or led a band of ecstatic children through some city streets. Who was this man of warmth and wisdom?

'That's Emomali Rahman,' said a thirty-something female passenger who had been watching me. 'He's the president of Tajikistan.'

'*Rahman.*' I had read about him. 'Is he a good president?'

'Of course,' said the lady. She repeated my question to the other passengers, and they all nodded.

Rahman has ruled this nation, virtually unopposed, since 1992. The first five years of his presidency saw a bitter civil war virtually tear the country apart. Up to 100,000 people were killed and over a million displaced. Militants from the country's Gorno-Badakhshan region, the main opposition fighting the government, were pacified after the war by being granted autonomy over their mountainous province in the east. My journey would lead through the western Rahman-heartlands of the country, where a solitary and notoriously dangerous road leads south through the mountains.

Before that though, I would need to spend the night in Tajikistan's second city, Khojand, where I shortly disembarked.

'Mister, mister,' shouted the lady from the bus. 'Welcome to Tajikistan. My name is Lila. I wondered if I can help you?' Lila wore a blue headscarf and had a bright, smiling face.

'My name's Oli,' we shook hands. 'I'm looking for a place to stay the night in Khojand.'

Lila tipped her head, then flashed her eyes and grabbed me by the arm. 'Follow me!'

She led me through a heaving bazaar and made a brief phone call. As we went, I noticed that people were watching us with particular curiosity. *'Have you seen the people?'* asked Lila, with a daring smile. 'It's very strange for them to see a local woman with a foreign man. Tajikistan is a very orthodox country. Men and women do not walk together in the street. Even if they are married, it is unusual to see this. But I don't mind.'

'Me neither, Lila, I'm used to it now.'

'This way,' said Lila, pointing up a stairwell which led into an apartment block. I followed her up to the fifth floor, where a slight and fidgety man was waiting. We shook hands, but his gaze twisted awkwardly.

'It's ok,' said Lila. 'This is my friend. He usually rents out this apartment, but right now it's empty. You are welcome to use it for the night, if you like?'

The man unlocked a steel outer door, then the wooden door within. Inside was a very large single bedroom, a kitchen and bathroom. The man simply dropped the key into my hand and shifted back into the stairwell.

'So,' I frowned at Lila, 'that's it?'

'That's it,' she smiled. 'Leave the key on the gas meter when you leave. Here's my number. Call me if you need anything. And have a great stay in Tajikistan!'

Thanking Lila before she left, I dropped my bags and looked out across the city. I was puzzled, but I felt like a king! I celebrated my good fortune with a giant plate of shashlik; succulent meat kebabs, and a regional staple. My joy was short-lived though, as I finally received a calling, but not the kind I had asked for. It was an eager dash back to my apartment.

As instructed, I left the key, along with a few Tajik Somoni, on the gas meter the next morning. It seemed an age since I had last climbed a mountain, and cabin-fever was kicking in once again. Located directly between Khojand and the capital city, Dushanbe, lie the towering Fann mountains which rise over 5500m. Boundless tempting climbs lay amongst them, but seven days of heavy snow left me feeling uncertain.

'South, to Dushanbe,' I said, to a group of flat-caps.

'Nyet, nyet,' they grumbled.

One man stepped forward and gestured falling snow and whistling winds, then finished with a vigorous shiver.

I understood what he meant, but I held out my hands. I needed to go south.

Doubtful, but happy to help, the men led me around the taxi rank, and called out, 'Dushanbe! Dushanbe!'

Most of the flat-caps shook their heads too, until we arrived a gleaming black pick-up truck, whose driver was loading cargo on the roof-racks. He turned and saw me. 'Dushanbe?'

'Dushanbe,' I replied. We bargained a price, and the driver hauled my bag onto the roof. Three young men soon filled the remaining seats. It should have been no more than a six-hour journey to the capital. I had located some provisional climbs in the Fann mountains, but the trailhead lay twenty-five miles off the highway on a dead-end mountain track. I planned to observe the mountain conditions from the road, and make a call as we travelled south.

We were soon surrounded by blizzard-beaten mountains and a dense fog rolled in. The snow on the roadside was over a metre deep in places. Our progress slowed with the traffic, and as we reached the remotest stretch of the highway, all cars came to a halt. A line of cars extended for a few hundred yards up to a police barricade. Thereafter, snow ploughs were working in the distance to tunnel through a five-metre deep avalanche which had buried the road.

We waited, and waited. I shared what food I had, and we were soon out of water. The driver left the engine off to conserve fuel, and the temperature inside the car fell below 0°C. In the recent past, colossal avalanches here have buried cars and taken dozens of lives. Occasionally, we heard thunderous echoes through the valleys. The mountains were so deeply laden with snow that the weight was too much. I gazed up the roadside mountain which soared into the fog and realised that we were like sitting ducks. It would be suicidal for me to wander alone into the mountains now. I decided to continue to Dushanbe, if we could make it that far.

It took six hours until the police beckoned the first car. We crept along the road through channels ploughed through a dozen fallen avalanches. At dusk, an impending tunnel promised a clear run, but this was Anzob's infamous Tunnel of Death: a three-mile long, unventilated, barely lit, dreadfully potholed and partially flooded tunnel below a mountain, which is said to have claimed several lives through carbon monoxide poisoning. Shortly, and predictably, as we steered through the tunnel, the traffic stopped once again. We were trapped, and the air was black with fumes. We could not turn back. We could not go forward. If we left the car, we would need to walk for over a mile through noxious gas. It was the most uncomfortable half an hour of my trip so far.

At midnight, after fifteen hours on the road, we finally reached Dushanbe, as a torrential downpour was sweeping through the streets. Something didn't feel right. This was a capital city, home to a million people, but it was palpably quiet. There were no people around whatsoever, and barely another car went by. My driver left me on the northern edge of the city. I approached a lone taxi nearby and asked for a ride towards the southern suburbs where I was staying.

We drove five-hundred yards until we reached a junction. Figures showed through the haze. They were standing in the road, motionless and staring straight at us. They each carried large assault rifles. The men ordered my taxi to stop, and six soldiers surrounded the car. They paused. The window wipers screeched. Huge raindrops bounced off the soldiers' trench coats and their eyes hid in the shadows below their helmets. They studied us for a moment, and then ordered my driver out of the taxi.

I remained under scrutiny, remembering the tale I'd heard of a traveller being robbed at gunpoint by police in this city. I could now hear a soldier shouting at my driver as they stood behind the car. A fist tapped against my window, 'Passport.'

I opened the door and handed them my passport. The soldiers huddled around, but returned it without asking any questions. They searched the car, scolded the driver once more, and then, with relief, let us continue. I felt like I'd arrived in Nazi Germany, I tried to ask my driver what was happening, but he was sulking and angry. We drove through two more checkpoints on our way. Each time, the driver was ordered out, our IDs were checked, and the car was searched. We eventually reached some backstreets and found the steel gates of the only hostel in town.

I hammered on the gates, and a studious young man appeared. 'You must be Oliver. Welcome.'

I followed him across an open courtyard and into a statuesque building with stone columns and a large balcony. Within, the hostel was warm and homely, a true oasis for a weary traveller.

'What's happening in Dushanbe tonight?' I asked. 'There are no cars or people. The roads are full of checkpoints.'

'Yes,' replied the man, 'It is because Rahman is away. He is visiting the United Arab Emirates, so there is a curfew until he returns, and social media has been blocked.'

'But why?'

'In a country like Tajikistan, when the President is gone, the seat of power is empty. There are certain groups of people who will try to take that seat of power when they have the chance, if you understand what I mean?' I took the thought to my dorm room, where for now, I was just happy to get some rest.

I awoke in a different place. Dushanbe by day was a colourful, bustling, friendly city, with parklands, golden statues, grandiose buildings, museums, and a bold central boulevard. I took in the city sights on a walk to the embassy of Turkmenistan, where I applied for my final outstanding visa.

Back in the hostel that night, I was happy to find a collective of regional travellers, and it was then that I met a man named Jawid. Unassuming, in jeans, trainers, and an Adidas tracksuit top, Jawid was an Afghan in his late-thirties, but he spoke with a tough London accent. His jaw was cloaked in dark stubble, and he had a good collection of scars on his face. There was something about Jawid which struck me at once. He was generally inexpressive, but laughed when he found amusement in something. He was independent, and would come and go when he pleased. And he was appreciative, for the slightest thing anybody did for him.

An instinct told me Jawid had a story to tell, so when he asked me to join him for a beer that night, I was eager to oblige. We happened upon an Irish bar on the main boulevard. It was filled with ex-pats, diplomats and local students. There was some European football on the TV, and a lively atmosphere, but it soon became background noise.

'I was nineteen when the Taliban attacks began.' Jawid stared into his half-drunk pint of beer and took a drag from his cigarette. 'I was a medical student at the University of Kabul. It was always my dream to go into medicine, but soon, because of the fighting, the University was shut down. The city had become too dangerous. My parents fled into Pakistan. My brothers wanted to stay in Kabul. I wanted to get out. I decided to travel to Europe. I made it across the border into Iran, but twice I was caught and returned to Afghanistan. On my third attempt, in Turkey, I remember sleeping rough with a group of other asylum seekers, Iraqis and Afghans. We were caught by the local police and taken to the police station. I knew they would deport us. So I went to the toilet and escaped through the window.'

'You managed to escape?'

'Yeah,' Jawid chuckled.

'What happened to the others?'

'I don't know. I guess they got sent back.'

'And how were you surviving? How were you getting around?'

'Sometimes I'd hitch rides. Sometimes I'd just walk. Then I would beg for money and sleep rough, or pick up little jobs here and there. I worked in a factory for a while in Turkey.'

'And how long did it take?'

'Three years,' Jawid looked back into his beer, 'it took me three years to reach England.'

'That's an incredible story, Jawid.'

'Pretty crazy, huh, but it doesn't end there. As soon as I arrived at the UK border, I requested asylum, and was taken to stay in London. But for ten years, I was unable to work, unable to leave the country, unable to see my family. *Ten years.* All the while, my friends were being killed in Kabul. Sometimes I felt trapped, and sometimes I wished I'd never left my family. When my asylum was finally granted, I was the happiest man alive. Now I've got a British passport. I worked for a couple of years as a bricklayer in London, and I then decided it was time to see my family again.'

'So you flew back to Kabul?'

'No,' said Jawid, 'I cycled. I cycled for three months, retracing my journey through Europe and Asia, but this time as a legal citizen. I wanted to raise money for the War Child charity, but I don't know so many people with money, so I couldn't raise very much. When I finally arrived in Kabul, it was the first time I'd seen my family in sixteen years. Imagine that.' Jawid tapped his cigarette in the ash tray and watched a coil of smoke rise past his face.

'And what now for you, Jawid? Would you ever like to study medicine again?'

Jawid sighed. 'That was my dream, but it's too late for me now, and sometimes it feels like my life has been wasted. No, I'll just keep on doing what I'm doing, making money where I can, and one day I may return to Afghanistan. To be honest, I'm just happy to be a free man.'

We each sat back in silence for a couple of minutes. Jawid may not have thought it himself, but I knew that I had encountered a truly special man; indeed, one of the most inspiring people I've ever met. He possessed a plucky, courageous, rousing spirit which made him stop at nothing to gain the freedom for himself that every human on earth deserves. Holding his story in my mind ever since, one is no longer so quick to complain about the hard times.

During the following day, Jawid and I, along with two Iranian travellers, Hamid and Mehdi, were whisked into a wonderful cultural vortex. After a breakfast of local cuisine, we visited the nearby ancient fort and madrasah of Hissar, where we met a group of rough horsemen training for the sport of Buzkashi. This game, regionally adored, involves two teams on horseback and a large field. Each team must battle to carry the carcass of a headless goat into the opposition's goal area. The game is not only gruesome, but violently physical, with broken bones and lacerations commonplace. We were all keen to watch a game of Buzkashi, but no locals seemed certain when the next fixture would be held.

We returned to Dushanbe to visit the imposing national museum, situated by a manicured park which includes the world's second largest flagpole, the world's largest tea house, the majestically named Palace of Nations, and a towering collection of ostentatious statues and stone buildings. These were not the kind of sights I expected to see in one of the poorest nations in Asia. Nonetheless, the museum was set to offer me an intriguing tip-off. In a cavernous room describing the geography of Tajikistan, I noticed a tiny placard which contained but a single sentence:

'*Istoriko Natural Park (Shirkent): The aim of creations of the park is preserving the natural monument, dinosaur, ancient metallurgy and mining of rare species, Tian Shan brown bear, golden eagle, Tibet ulara and rare species of flora.*'

The poor translation made little sense, but I found myself repeating one word, 'Dinosaur.' That evening, further research revealed a couple of old web pages explaining the discovery of dinosaur footprints by a Russian archaeologist in 1963. I found no maps, and no detailed indication of where the footprints lay. Yet the allure of a little known mountain village, numberless peaks, and a prehistoric relic had enraptured me. Could this, I wondered, be the calling I was waiting for?

13

'Nowruz Mubarak!' beamed Hamid and Mehdi the next morning.

'It means happy new year,' Mehdi added.

'Today is the Persian New Year,' said Hamid, 'and it marks the first day of spring.'

'Nowruz Mubarak!' I replied. Winter was finally waning.

'There's a big festival at the Hippodrome today,' said Jawid, 'we're leaving in ten minutes. Are you coming with us?'

'Of course!'

There was an incredible atmosphere on the city streets. The girls were clothed in vibrant dresses, and some carried flowers. The men and boys wore suits and traditional hats. As we neared the hippodrome, huge clusters of dancers spiralled around traditional bands. They played horns, drums, flutes and unusual string instruments. The hippodrome was a vast swathe of grass, encircled by a broad horse track. In the centre of this, there was a magnificent show underway for the watching dignitaries. Outside the carnival, young men fought in fiery wrestling matches or scrambled around huge vats of plov. The girls whirled and danced. The perimeter of the Hippodrome was surrounded by hundreds of colourful stalls, displaying the finest foods and wares of local businesses.

As foreigners, we were constantly mobbed by well-wishers and proud cooks, who offered us all the finest regional delights. I couldn't walk five paces without being asked for a picture, and I was delighted to oblige. This was, bizarrely, the third New Year I had celebrated since the start of my expedition, and I was loving every second of it. Revellers believe that their actions on New Year's Day are representative of how their year ahead will unfold. So kindness, generosity and hospitality are endlessly displayed.

One moment, I strayed too close to the dancing hordes, and was inevitably thrust into the centre of the spiralling circle. A mass of onlookers rushed to watch. This was my moment. I imitated the best dancers I could see. I shimmied my chest, flailed my arms, and grooved my head from side to side. The crowd laughed and clapped and cheered. Then, children started stuffing money into my hands; one Somoni here, three Somoni there. *What were they doing?*

With a final flourish, I bowed to my watching fans and withdrew from the circle.

'Well done, Oli!' said Mehdi, clutching my shoulder.

'Thank you,' I laughed. 'But why did they give me money?'

'Ah, that is a sign of gratitude. In Persian culture, if somebody entertains the crowd at a party, then the crowd give them money to say thanks. You must have impressed them!'

I replied with laughter. Never in the history of my life have my dancing skills impressed a soul.

We enjoyed the celebrations until the evening, when we retreated to the hostel for a goodbye meal. Tomorrow we each would part ways. On our return, I found a familiar face on the outside porch.

'Sam?'

'Oh, hi, Oli. How are you doing?'

It was the Malaysian man I had met in Bishkek, who told me about getting robbed at gunpoint. 'I'm great thanks, what brings you back to Dushanbe?'

'Sorry, one moment.' Sam's phone was ringing. He gestured to a young lady standing next to him. 'This is Zarrina, my translator.'

Sam took his call as I greeted Zarrina. She was professionally dressed, and spoke with impeccable English. 'I think I saw you at the hippodrome today. Yes, you were dancing among a group of people.'

'I'm sorry you had to witness that.'

Zarrina laughed. 'How do you like Tajikistan?'

'I love this country. Everyone I have met are warm and friendly, but I had my doubts before I arrived. I met your friend, Sam, in Bishkek. He warned me to watch out for the police after they took his money.'

'Sam's not my friend.' Said Zarrina. 'I've been working for him for five days, but because he isn't getting any business here in Dushanbe, he says he won't pay me. I'm an interpreter, not a saleswoman!'

'That's ridiculous. You shouldn't work for him anymore. Do you want me to say something to him?'

'No, no, I will speak with my boss. I don't want to work for Sam anymore. I want to go home and see my family, to celebrate the New Year with them. He wouldn't let me go today.'

'Well, tomorrow you should go. Where is home, anyway?'

'Have you heard of Tursunzoda?'

'*Tursunzoda?* Isn't that near Shirkent?'

'How do you know about Shirkent?' Zarrina frowned. 'It's a tiny village in the mountains.'

'Because of the dinosaur footprints. I was planning to go there tomorrow and see what I can find.'

'Then we can go together!' Zarrina smiled. 'I have family in Shirkent so maybe I can help you.'

'That's amazing!'

'Sam's coming,' she whispered. 'Meet me at Zarnisar Bazaar tomorrow at 9am.'

'See you there.'

Jawid, Mehdi, Hamid and I shared a lavish dinner of shashlik, salad, eggs, cheese, bread and Persian tea. They were cultured, interesting and intelligent people, who I was sorry to say goodbye to. We vowed to keep in touch, and Mehdi gave me an ornate Iranian tile as a parting gift.

At 8.45am the next morning, I was laden with bags once again and ready to hit the road. Our meeting place was a transit hub in the western suburbs of the city. I fended off the flat-caps until Zarrina arrived at precisely 9am. 'We're going to Shirkent!' she cried. 'I've spoken to my Aunt. She's happy to let you stay at their farm in the village. Everyone's very excited to meet you.'

We travelled for an hour to the industrial town of Tursunzoda. The town lies on a plain south of the Hissar Mountain Range, where Shirkent is located. Zarrina had arranged for a friend to collect us from the taxi stop, informing me that he is the son of Tursunzoda's former mayor. Fedya, aged twenty, arrived in a pristine black Audi, and offered to take us for some tea at his house.

We arrived at a gated mansion, with a security box outside. The guard opened the gate, and Fedya cruised into a paved courtyard. 'This, my house,' said Fedya, before pointing around. 'This, my mother, this, my maid, and he is my sister.'

'He's still learning English,' Zarrina mouthed.

'It's a beautiful house.' I said to Fedya

'Yeas,' Fedya nodded, but I don't think he understood me. 'Come and eat some tea.'

He led Zarrina and I to an opulent summerhouse, and poured freshly brewed tea into three fine china cups.

'You two should talk,' said Zarrina. 'Fedya needs to improve his English!'

After some probing and confusion, I found a topic which finally provided a common language. So we played a long-winded and inconsequential game of footballer name tennis, which went something like this:

'Ronaldo?'

'Yes. Rooney?'

'Yes. Messi?'

'Yes. Giggs?'

'No, no. Oh, yes! Giggs!'

Fortunately, we were rescued as two of Fedya's friends arrived; Bobo and Olim. The latter spoke good English, and was interested in my quest towards Shirkent. I told him all about the museum, and the archaeologist, and the footprints.'

I expected fascination, rapture and excitement, but Olim replied in a comforting manner, as though revealing to me the truth about Father Christmas; 'Oli, they don't exist.'

'I've read about them, and seen pictures.'

'No, Oli,' he shook his head, 'they don't exist.'

Olim relayed our debate to Fedya and Bobo. Bobo shrugged his shoulders, but Fedya starting wagging his finger with a sudden vigour. 'Yeas, Oli, yeas, yeas!' Then he stopped, recoiled his finger, and shook his head. 'No, no.'

'Right,' I said. 'Should we head to Shirkent now, Zarrina?'

'Let's go.'

Fedya offered to take us there, and his friends came too. We stopped en route to view a hidden waterfall, where Olim's family owned a utopian cherry tree plantation. I thanked Fedya for the ride, and they all insisted I return to Tursunzoda with the tale from my fossil hunt.

I had arrived in a humble farming community which stretched alongside a wide glacial riverbed. The surrounding hills were strikingly green, and contained mesmerising rock formations. A backdrop of ice white and azure depicted the distant mountains and sky. I could sense both the simplicity of this place, and the stir that my arrival had caused; with villagers peering at me through the window of Fedya's sleek saloon.

Zarrina led me through the gateway of a small farmyard plot by the river. Within, there was a barn, a few crops and trees, and then a couple of small buildings. Chickens dashed from beneath out feet, and we heard the mooing of a nearby cow. A little head emerged from the barn. It was a young boy, who yelled something, pointed, and then disappeared. An elderly lady emerged in his place.

'Zarrina!' She hustled over, and gave Zarrina a kiss.

Zarrina introduced me to her aunt. 'Salom!' I shook her hand. Yet worry was etched on the face of this lady. She beckoned us to follow her into the barn.

Here we saw a punch-drunk new-born calf, and behind it, an almost lifeless cow whose innards were hanging out from behind.

A young man was knelt nearby, while an older gentleman, with a neat beard, examined the cow. Zarrina translated what the young man told her. 'This is Mani, my cousin. He says that the cow gave birth just a few hours ago, but now she's very sick. This is my family's only cow, and the vet doesn't know if she'll survive.'

Mani was mournful. He rubbed the cow's stomach and shook his head.

With a deep huff, the aunt clapped her hands and asked us to follow. Across the way, below a shelter, four ladies were seated around a traditional Tajik table; a large but short-legged furnishing, which stands on a raised block with cushions for people to sit on. These ladies were Zarrina's mother, and her three cousins in their twenties. Like the aunt, they were all attired in long, colourful dresses and headscarves. Each of the younger ladies wore a traditional black line joining their eyebrows; a sign of beauty in Tajikistan. They were shy at first; tittering, whispering, and glancing away. Zarrina told me that they had never seen a foreigner in their village before.

We shared a banquet of delectable home-grown fare, and as Mani returned from the barn, saying that the cow was getting better, the mood became one of great excitement.

'They want to take you around the village,' said Zarrina. 'Parisa and Seema want to show you their houses, and to cook a meal for you.

So we trooped through the village, the girls smiling ceaselessly, and hyper with jubilation. My long tour of Shirkent became a festival of food and hospitality, as I was invited in four separate houses for tea, bread, soup, plov, cakes, homemade jam and juice, fruits, nuts and more, until I could barely waddle. The Tajik dining experience is fashioned for conversation. Seated on the ground, guests encircle countless bowls of food on the floor in the centre. Generous hands criss-cross as the bounty is shared with all. I quickly learned the subtle rhythm of Tajik feasting, and felt wholly accepted within the group. Yet, in one less than dignified moment, I realised I was cross-legged with a tear in my trouser-crotch and almost revealing my prize possessions to a trio of beaming grannies.

As I met more of Zarrina's relatives, particularly the young children, I developed two unfortunate nicknames: Freckle and Mr Bean. At dusk we climbed a small nearby hill, the girls rolling with laugher as they slipped in their sandals. When we reached the top, and watched the sunset, the female cousins announced that this was the best day of their lives.

Zarrina had told me that her uncle works six days a week in the local aluminium plant, earning just US$100 per month to support his family of six. My day in Shirkent had left me with an overwhelming sense of gratitude. By international standards, this family was deeply impoverished, yet they had welcomed me like a relative, and fed me like a king. Theirs was one of the most striking acts of kindness I have ever received and I cannot overstate my appreciation.

There was good news at dawn. The cow was walking and grazing once again. Mani was delighted, and declared that he would join my quest to find the dinosaur footprints. Zarrina wished to come too, along with Mani's younger brother, Kia, and their friend, Neda. We breakfasted with Zarrina's uncle, who, via Zarrina, told me a story:

'I told my friends at work that I had a man from England staying in my house. They replied, *'That's impossible! Impossible!'* Nobody could believe me,' he laughed. 'Oli, I want to thank you for visiting me and my family. In all my life, I never thought anything like this would happen to me, *to me!* This will be a good year for my family, and I wish to name our new-born calf after you!'

I replied that the honour was all mine, and I know to this day that a remote mountain village in Tajikistan now contains a cow named Mr Bean.

Everybody was very excited by our adventure. The family had heard rumours of the dinosaur footprints, but nobody had ever seen, or even knew the whereabouts of, these relics. Some, like Olim, even doubted their existence. Zarrina's aunt had prepared an obligatory feast to fill our packs, and we set out shortly after sunrise. The lady cousins cheered as we left 'Take a picture if you find them!'

Our noses took us north through Shirkent and into the mountains. The village stretched along a narrow valley, with occasional houses spread across undulating plots of farmland. We occasionally saw shepherds in the hills, and farmers carrying hand-rolled bales of hay. Bees buzzed around beekeepers' hives, cows and goats grazed the fields, and children played down by the riverbed. This was a true idyll: unspoiled and serene.

There is a pleasant custom in Central Asia, and particularly in Tajikistan. When greeting somebody or offering something, one should concurrently touch one's heart to show respect and sincerity. This gesture is contagious. Chattering old villagers would say 'Salom,' and clutch their chest. Children would do likewise as they came to shake my hand. I was falling in love with this place.

We walked for an hour, guided by the vaguely pointing fingers of various locals, until we reached the house of a giant: hands like tree roots and a head like a boulder. He eyed us up and down.

'We're looking for the dinosaur footprints,' said Mani.

The giant's head lurched. His fingers scratched the crack between his chin. 'There's only one man who knows where they are. He lives in the last house across the river. Watch out for his dogs.'

The giant sent us on our way, and lurched back into his dwelling. We crossed a bridge of sticks and the frosty water whizzed beneath our feet. Two dogs bolted at once, dashing towards us, teeth bared, until the chains went tight around their necks. A frowning man emerged, shadowed by his two bleary-eyed sons. It seemed he was our final gatekeeper. He pacified the dogs, and came to meet us.

'I understand you know about the footprints,' said Mani.

The gatekeeper continued to frown. 'I can take you there, but it will cost you.' He examined our group, and me especially. 'One-Hundred Somoni each, and I'll take you to the footprints.'

Mani considered his strategy. 'This foreigner is our friend and a guest in our community. We don't have enough money to pay, and we can find our own way to the footprints. We just need a little help.'

The gatekeeper sighed, and his sons borrowed his frown. 'Ok.' He crouched and began to draw a map in the ground of where we ought to go. He described the path in further detail to Mani, who would become our leader with his new-found knowledge.

We thanked the man, then veered off the main river, and along an enticing tributary. The further we walked, the more it felt like we were entering a lost world. There were millennia old seabeds frozen in time on the mountainside, and fossilised shells in almost every rock. Kia and Neda found a fist-sized ammonite, which they carried as a good luck charm. We crossed the river once again, and began to ascend the left side of the valley. Together we traversed a winding grassy slope, crossing interesting rock formations and rambling streams, and always scanning for the footprints.

We passed through a section of dry undergrowth and heard the desperate cries of a nearby bird. It was flapping in a pool of dust; its leg caught on wire. As we moved to investigate, two men in camouflage jumped from the bushes. One man grabbed the bird and held it under his arm. They were trappers, and they each approached with a hand on their heart. They had knives on their hips, wire nooses on their arms, and water canisters dangling from their shoulders.

'Salom,' whispered the man with the bird. It looked like some kind of grouse. He held it out so we could stroke it. Zarrina winced. The man held his finger to his lips, hinting that he'd set more traps nearby. Without another word, the men retreated into the scrub and we continued on our way.

By now, we had been walking and searching for around five hours and the midday temperature was surprisingly hot. We had almost reached the base of a steep cauldron-like cliff, which marked the end of the valley. I was starting to wonder whether the footprints had eluded us. There were crags everywhere we looked. Mani seemed unsure of where we ought to go, and Zarrina, protesting that she was unfit, said she did not want to continue any further. Kia and Neda, meanwhile, full of energy, had dashed ahead.

We paused to fill our water bottles in a stream, and give Zarrina a moment in the shade. Then, there was a shout from beyond, 'In co! In co!'

'That's Kia,' said Zarrina, 'he says 'Here! Here!''

We ran to find them, scrambled down some rocks and across a stream to a sweeping cliff face, almost fifty metres high. And then, in a moment of sheer astonishment, all was revealed. Along this cliff, dozens of fossilised footprints could be seen, each print half a metre long and containing three bulbous toes and a heel. The prints extended across a large section of the cliff so vividly that one could envisage the prehistoric beasts roaming these lands in an age long, long ago. So long ago indeed, that the plains on which they wandered have since been uplifted to become glorious mountains. Beholding this sight, following my serendipitous meeting with Zarrina, my carnival welcome into Shirkent, and our long, uncertain journey through the mountains made this one the of the most astounding moments of both my expedition and my life.

Kia, Neda and I climbed part way up the cliff to examine the footprints more closely, before retreating for lunch in the valley. Kia entertained us by describing his knowledge of the English language, which extended to four words: hello, goodbye, OK, and cheese.

Our success left me high on energy, and I remembered my unfinished business. Beyond the cliffs and in the distance, I scoped a tempting peak, whose approach promised scree slopes and scrambling. There could be no other peak. It may not be the biggest, nor the snowiest, but this was to be my Tajik mountain.

Neda opted to join me, and the others agreed to relax by the cliff until our return. It was a fun ascent over mixed terrain. We found swathes of wild spring onions, and then the footprint of an altogether different creature: a Tien Shan brown bear. Neda stopped to rest while I continued to reach the summit after an hour of fast and light climbing. Despite only measuring 2010 metres, this nameless, unmapped peak was one of the most satisfying to ascend. It might be known, if the pleasure could be mine, as Dinosaur Peak.

This magical day would conclude with one final treat. After returning to the village and sharing our joy and photographs with the family, I was invited to join a most outlandish celebration.

We followed the trail of drumming and singing, and a plume of smoke which rose from a nearby courtyard into the night sky. Within, a local family welcomed us with excited whoops. They danced around a vast cauldron over a fire, which one lady stirred with a six-foot ladle. The fire, the sole light source in courtyard, illuminated a man beating on a hand drum, and children and ladies twirling, hollering and dancing.

'This is a sumanak party!' said Zarrina. 'It happens only in Tajikistan and only during Nowruz. Inside the pot is a sweet mixture of wheat juices and water, plus walnuts and small rocks for good luck. The mixture must be stirred for twenty-four hours until it's thick like honey. And when somebody makes sumanak, all the village is invited. It becomes a festival. People dance and sing through the night.'

I was whisked towards the bubbling cauldron, where I stirred and voiced my wishes for the year ahead, as tradition dictates. I offered my finest moves on the dusty dancefloor as the hours drifted along. Later, the drum was placed in my hands, and all the villagers cheered for me to sing an English song.

'Help me, Zarrina. I can't think of anything!'

'How about,' she mused, 'the national anthem?'

And so, beside a fire in a scarcely-visited mountain village in Tajikistan, surrounded by applauding locals, I drummed and sang 'God Save The Queen,' believing that nothing could ever tear me from this rapturous state.

14

'When you write your book,' said Zarrina's uncle to me, 'remember to tell the world about Shirkent!'

'You have my word.' We shook hands, and I thanked him one final time for his hospitality.

The lady cousins gifted me some fine Tajik silks, while Zarrina's aunt gave me an enormous jar of sumanak. 'You need to keep it cold and eat it all within two days.' Challenge wagered, I placed the jar in my rucksack. Despite their poverty, and their boundless kindness, Zarrina's family would accept nothing in return.

The aunt's two-year old granddaughter, Aisha, who had spent the duration of my visit kissing my cheek and saying 'I love you,' cried as I climbed into Mani's old car. With great sorrow but enduring memories, I waved goodbye to my adoptive Tajik family, and we cruised back down the valley towards Tursanzoda.

This town lay just a few miles from the Uzbek border, which I was eager to cross at once, with the prospect of a long journey ahead. However, when Zarrina and I converged with Fedya, Olim and Bo, a party invitation was extended my way, and I felt it was too rude not to accept. I suppose one final feast was fitting before I left this country behind. My short journey through Tajikistan had rendered me besotted. Kindness perpetuates the bloodstreams of its people, as grandeur does its mountains. This wild, rugged republic possessed everything I hoped to find on my journey and more, and I know beyond doubt that Tajikistan and I will one day reconvene.

At the party, I dumbfounded Olim with pictures of the dinosaur footprints, and made a friend out of Fedya with the translated tales of my journey so far. I owed immense debt to Zarrina in particular, who had orchestrated my prehistoric quest, but I asked her for one final favour before my departure.

It had been several days since I last spoke to Emma, and as I aimed towards an undeveloped Uzbek village, I did not know when we would talk again. Zarrina lent me her phone, and I sent Emma this message:

'On my way to the Uzbek border. Heading for the town of Boysun. Will be in touch again as soon as I can. Love you and miss you, Oli x.'

With nightfall approaching, I hadn't time to wait for a reply.

I said goodbye to my friends and took a shared taxi towards the seventh country of my expedition.

I was alone again and feeling invigorated. Only positivity remained in my mind, *almost.* There was, when I came to confront it, the slightest, measliest, pipsqueak of a concern tottering around in my head. Jawid had warned me that the Uzbek border guards can be somewhat overzealous in their duties, and that Uzbekistan's repressive, autocratic regime made the country rather different to its regional cousins. But then I shook my head. After my journey so far, this flicker of a doubt deserved but a flicker of attention.

The dusk was dark and damp. Swollen rainclouds converged overhead, and stole the daylight before its time had passed. A horizon of metal fencing centred on a near-deserted border post. The taxi dropped myself and two ladies at some concrete barricades, one hundred yards from the Tajik station.

A money-changer reeled through the drizzle, 'Dollar? Som? Somoni? Euro?'

'Nyet.'

The two ladies continued past the Tajik border guard after a short inspection, leaving me to face him alone. He was fleshy, shaven-headed man with divots in his brow. 'Passport.' He tapped his desk. I gave it to him. He glanced through. 'Immigration card.' He tapped his desk, but I shrugged my shoulders.

'I arrived at Isfara, from Kyrgyzstan. They didn't give me an immigration card. I don't have one.'

The guard's eyes inflated as he shook his head and tutted. He placed my passport back on his desk, and pointed towards Tajikistan.

'No,' I said, 'I can't go back. I need to enter Uzbekistan today!'

'No immigration card, no Uzbekistan.'

'It's not my fault. Contact the guards at Isfara if you need to.'

He leant forward and jabbed his finger at me, '*You* go back to Isfara. You cannot cross here. You, Uzbekistan, no!'

I paused for a moment, quietly seething, and anticipating, with immediate accuracy, what would happen next. After reclining, uninterested, the guard looked about him, and then across towards the concrete barricades. Nobody was around but he and I. He leant forward once again, and whispered, '*Money.*'

I laughed, 'No.'

He shrugged.

It was time to defeat this crook. 'I'm a guest in your country,' I said. 'and I love Tajikistan. When I return to England, I will tell all my friends how great your country is, and you want to bribe me? Are you really going to let your country down? Let me go, right now!'

He stared a moment more, then took my passport and delivered his stamp. 'Goodbye.'

Bastard.

I dashed across the rainy no-mans-land and towards the Uzbek frontier. Their border post inside was sterile, with white floors, white walls, white ceilings and white benches. Ahead, there were three white stalls with glass fronts and green-uniformed officers within. The officer in the centre summoned me forth. He was courteous, eloquent, and smiling – my doubts had been unfounded. He checked my visa, asked some simple questions, and stamped my passport.

'Welcome to Uzbekistan, sir.'

I felt rather stunned. Boysun, my destined mountain village, was now just a couple of hours away. I continued into a second white room, which contained some immigration forms – a bureaucratic staple. I completed the form, signed my name, and continued buoyantly into a third white room.

This room was much bigger than the others. It comprised some large, empty desks, a couple of computer-bound guards, and some sections of white screening. A diminutive guard with protruding eyes and a tight jaw approached. He took my immigration form and handed it to his colleague at the computer, before asking me to place my bags on a desk.

'Camera, phone, laptop.' He outstretched his hand, and bulged his eyes at me. 'Give me.'

Unsettled, I gave him my phone, two cameras and laptop.

'Phone password.' He pointed the screen at me.

'Why?' I scowled.

He sucked his teeth. 'Inspection. Password.'

I'd been warned this might happen, but I had nothing to hide. I entered my password, and he began scrolling through my phone. Meanwhile, his corpulent colleague browsed through the photographs on my cameras, then the files on my laptop.

I was angry. How could they do they do this to visitors of their country?

Popeye eventually returned my phone, and led me behind

some screening. If he was planning on doing a cavity search, I swore I'd prod him in the eyeballs. He emptied my pockets, patted me down, and left my honour intact.

Popeye led me back to his colleague, who had finished plundering my privacy. It seemed I was free to go, until Olive Oyl arrived. 'Sir, I need to check your bags.' She was a bony lady in her thirties with a tight ponytail and a sorrowful face. She spoke better English than the others, and with a high-pitched voice.

Olive Oyl began her search, sifting through my clothes, toiletries, charging cables, sleeping bag, mountaineering gear, shoes, spare food, the jar of sumanak, and a file of important documents. She swept through everything, not leaving a single pocket unzipped or unchecked. She wore black shoes and black tights, then a narrow green skirt which finished precisely at her knee. She wore a white shirt, green jacket and tie, a smidgeon of make-up and name badge which revealed her name was Larina. She searched until she arrived at my first aid kit, stored and waterproofed inside two clear food bags.

'Sir, do you have any strong drugs or medication?'

'No, nothing.'

'Open the bag.'

I unknotted the first aid kit, and watched her nail-bitten fingers sifter and sort, until, they flinched. Larina collected two packets of co-codamol tablets and held them before her eyes.

'Mr-,' she looked at my passport, 'Oliver.'

'Yes?'

'Follow me.'

'Is there a problem?'

Larina's face was blank. 'Small problem. Bring your bags.'

I was led outside for my first grey glimpse of Uzbekistan. Armed soldiers were stationed across the border gates in the near distance, but I was taken to a two-story rectangular building. Inside, camouflage-clad soldiers peered at me from a crowded office. Larina led me upstairs, along an unlit corridor, and into an interrogation room. She seated me across the desk from a square-jawed officer, and positioned herself beside him.

I was ignored completely for the next thirty minutes, as Larina and Jaws spoke in Uzbek, Larina came and went, and Jaws tapped on his computer. Finally, Larina returned with the tablets and a skinny man with weary eyes and a sharp nose, who looked remarkably like Yoqub, the overbearing Uzbek man I had met in Almaty. This man took some photographs of me, and of the tablets which were placed before me, and then he left.

'Mr Oliver,' Larina started, shuffling some papers, 'do you know that co-codamol -codeine - is an illegal narcotic in Uzbekistan?'

'I had no idea.'

'But this cannot be a surprise to you. Codeine is illegal in many countries.'

'This was an innocent mistake. I was using them as a painkiller. I got them in the UK, and-.'

'But you're not in your country anymore, Mr Oliver.'

Larina's response was blunt, but of course I knew that she was right. My passport was stamped. My immigration card was signed. I was now wholly and legally in the jurisdiction of Uzbekistan. There was nothing I could do.

A three-hour interrogation ensued, where Larina asked about my reason for travel, my knee problem, my co-codamol dosage, and much more. Jaws, barely glancing at me, typed out my responses on his computer. Other soldiers would occasionally visit the interrogation room to observe their latest catch. Some seemed friendly, others, decidedly unpleasant. All the while, my racing mind was converging at the equation that illegal narcotics + a totalitarian state = goodbye life and hello prison. Finally, Larina's questions ended and Jaws stopped typing. They printed a number of papers, each written in Cyrillic script, and placed them before me.

'This is what will happen now, Mr Oliver,' said Larina. 'I will pass you a pen, and you will sign each of these papers. Signing these papers will make everything much easier.'

I left the pen where it lay after Larina slid it towards me. 'Before I sign *anything*, I need you to tell me what will happen to me.'

Larina inhaled. 'You will stay here tonight. After that, I do not know, and I do not want to say, but maybe, *maybe*, not prison.'

It was now 10pm and I could sense that Larina and Jaws were tired. That moment, I hatched a plan. A solitary option emerged that might just help me out of this predicament. Yet to act, I needed to stand my ground until the morning.

'Larina,' I returned, 'I have no idea what these papers say. I cannot read Cyrillic, and I refuse to sign anything tonight. Can you show me to where I will stay this evening?'

Jaws tensed his jaw, and I felt I'd gained some control over the situation. I was taken to a very basic room along the corridor, which contained only a bed, a desk and a chair. Then, asking if I was hungry, Larina led me to a canteen, where a dozen soldiers were gathered around a droning television, watching football highlights; Uzbekistan versus The Philippines. There was a ripple of chatter as I entered.

'My name is Ruslan,' a soldier sat beside me while I ate. 'What are you? An American? German?'

I looked up to greet a man with the body of a toddler. He had a blubbery face, a crystal-white shirt and chubby fingers.

'I'm English.'

'*English*,' Ruslan hissed. 'I like the English girls, but why don't they come here to Uzbekistan? I need an English girl to visit my border so I can marry them. Ruslan would give them a good life.' He patted his chest and chuckled. I ignored him. 'So you're the one with the drugs?'

'I don't have any drugs.'

Ruslan tutted. 'Which drugs are you bringing into my country?' His juvenile eyes stared through his flabby cheeks. He was the only soldier in the canteen who wore his cap, and I reckoned he was fresh out of training. '*I know, I know, I know, it's for the sex, isn't it? You brought Viagra, yes? I know, I know!*'

I gave him nothing but a glance.

Ruslan chuckled once more, and squeezed my shoulder. 'I speak good English, yes? Only Larina and I speak good English. If you want anything, you ask for Ruslan, OK? Ruslan will look after you.'

That evening, I watched over the clammy border post through the broken slats of my bedroom blind. Laughter and bickering echoed from the soldiers' dorm across the corridor. I had no phone signal, and I eventually gave up trying to guess the password for the station's Wi-Fi. Frustration and uncertainty weighed heavy on my mind. I should have learned that co-codamol was illegal here. But during the search, why couldn't Larina have just thrown the tablets in the bin and let me go? All this trouble, for a dozen little white pills. Twelve meagre pills intended to relive pain and now the root cause of my suffering. Twelve wretched little cretins whose extracted codeine weighed less than a tenth of a gram;

but a grain of sand. And how the implications of that grain of sand -
that infinitesimal, paltry little particle –were only just getting started.

'I want to speak to my embassy.'

Larina frowned. My demand had knocked her a little. She
shared some words with Jaws. 'And if you speak to your embassy,
then will you sign our papers?'

'Perhaps.'

Jaws upturned his palms, then Larina returned. 'Ok then, Mr
Oliver. You can make *one* phone call. But you have only three
minutes.'

They led me down to the main office, and sat me before an
old grey telephone. I had written down the phone number of the
British Embassy in Tashkent. It was time for stoic old Blighty to
come to my rescue. Let the Union Jack sail and the Red Arrows fly!
Let the fair green island liberate me from the shackles of
incarceration!

'Three minutes,' repeated Larina, as I picked up the phone
and began to dial.

It rang three times, and then, 'Hello, this is the British
Embassy in Tashkent -.'

'Hello, yes -.'

'- We are currently closed for the Easter weekend. The
Embassy will resume normal opening hours on Tuesday 29th March.
We apologise for any inconvenience. If you have an emergency, you
are advised to contact the American Embassy in Tashkent.' The
message ended with an unceremonious beep. The Red Arrows would
not fly.

It was the morning of Good Friday. A full four days would
pass before the embassy reopened, and as Larina removed the phone
from the desk before me, I realised that my master plan had failed. I
was now alone, and I alone would need to unshackle myself from
this mess. I protested to be given a second phone call, but my
argument was futile.

Larina and Jaws stood before me and asked with a renewed
harshness, 'Will you sign the papers or not?'

'You must understand,' I replied, 'I do not know what any of
these papers say, and so I do not know what I'm signing. I want to
get this over with as soon as possible and continue with my journey,
but until somebody can tell me exactly what's going to happen to
me, *no, I will not sign your papers.*'

'Ok, Mr Oliver. Then we must take you to Termez.'

15

By mid-morning, I was loaded onto a southbound bus, accompanied by Larina, Jaws, Ruslan and a number of other soldiers. They were taking me towards the southernmost point of Uzbekistan and to an ancient city on the Afghan border, Termez. The two-hour drive brought little conversation. Larina listened to blasting Uzbek pop music through her headphones. Jaws sat beside me, virtually motionless for the entire journey. Ruslan, meanwhile, was up top beside the driver, wearing his cap. Eventually, now far from any mountains, we reached a dusty and uninspiring place.

'We're taking you to the customs and border office, Mr Oliver. There's a lawyer and interpreter waiting for you.'

Larina, Jaws and I passed through an internal security gate and into an obligatory white room with an X-shaped table; shaped so, I figured, to be used for my forthcoming crucifixion. The lawyer was a short, spherical lady bejewelled in golden bracelets, and wearing two-inch purple fingernails. My interpreter was a smart, suited man with a neat haircut. He translated the discussion that ensued.

Larina began. 'We are here, Mr Oliver, so that we can finally complete your paperwork and move on with your case. If you have any questions, you may ask your lawyer. She will represent you now.'

My lawyer was flicking through the paperwork provided by Jaws. She peered over her gold-framed glasses when I asked, 'Have you represented anyone detained for possessing codeine before?'

'There have been a couple of travellers like you.'

'I need to understand what will happen to me.'

She shuffled the papers and removed her glasses. 'Mister, you have been detained for possessing an illegal narcotic. This is a serious problem. Your case must be taken to court, and a judge will decide your punishment on behalf of the state. This punishment might be a fine. It might be prison. I cannot say for certain. I will warn you though that there is a long backlog of cases at the moment, and it might be thirty days until your court hearing, during which time you will be held in jail.'

Jail? I couldn't go to jail. Me; a pasty-skinned, blonde-haired, bearded foreigner. Thirty days in prison on the Afghan border among Uzbekistan's vilest convicts and crooks. A place where torture and violence is more regular than breakfast, and all for a mildly pain-relieving little particle of codeine. I remember speaking to Meder, the drug-dealer in Bishkek. He said that if I go to prison, *they will kill me*! And what about Emma, and my family, and my wedding in less than four months' time. I could not go to jail.

I angled my head, and softened my tone, 'Are there any other options at all? I am on a long journey, and I need to continue towards home, towards my family. I'm willing to cooperate.'

'I suppose,' replied the lawyer, 'there could be a possibility, a *small* possibility, that the court will accept the early payment of a fine. If so, the matter could be finished more quickly.'

'If they allow it, how much is the fine?'

'It could be $1500 US Dollars, or $1000 Dollars. It sometimes depends how much money the accused person has available.'

'I must tell you,' I quickly lied, 'that I have very, very, little money available. Just a few hundred dollars left. I'm a young and poor traveller. I eat at street stalls and stay in cheap hostels.'

The lawyer wrestled in thought for a moment, as I maintained a mournful expression. 'I could see if they would accept $500, but if I ask for anything less, they may prefer to take you before the judge. But, Mister, in order for the court to consider an early fine, they must have all evidence, and all these statements,' she shook the papers, 'completed and signed.'

I could not know whether to trust what the lawyer was telling me, but I offered a calm reply, 'Ok.'

'There's one more thing,' said the lawyer, 'the evidence must show that you no longer have any codeine in your body. So you must provide a blood and urine sample today.'

I deemed that this was my only choice. I could wait for a court hearing, attempt to plead my innocence and be released free of charge, but I'd have been murdered in jail by then anyway. Handing $500 to a dictatorial state would not be pleasant, but my options were bleak, and I needed to act. I agreed to provide the required samples, and finally lent my signature to Jaws' papers.

Larina became my sole charge. She kept my passport in her handbag, but let me keep all my other possessions. We got a ride across the city with an off-duty solider to a small medical clinic, where I peed in a little cup, and had my veins jabbed by a sweaty doctor. After this, Larina relaxed a little. I spoke to her about her family. She was a single mother with two young children whom she was barely able to visit, and she was one of few female border guards in the country.

She took me to an Uzbek fast food restaurant to get a kebab. Its young customers seemed curious to see a foreigner eating lunch with a female official. I noticed their western style dress, and an absence of any symbols of religion. I knew Uzbekistan to be a strictly secular country, and read anecdotal reports of beards and headscarves being banned.

As we left, I asked Larina what would happen next.

'You will not stay in jail tonight, Mr Oliver. You will be allowed to stay in a hotel in Termez city, and not allowed to leave. I will keep your passport. You must know that if you try and leave the hotel and are caught by police without your passport, you will be in big trouble. You must not leave your room. Do you understand?'

'Yes.'

Tomorrow, hopefully, your samples will have been processed, and the court will have all the evidence they need. Then, your lawyer should find out whether the court will accept an early fine, or if you must wait for a court hearing. I will visit you in the morning with news.'

Larina delivered me to a deplorable hotel alongside a busy road in Termez. The receptionist was an angry woman with a mullet, and she handed me a key for room number 304. Larina explained to the receptionist that I was not to leave hotel, but left her phone number so that I could call if I needed anything.

My room comprised two single beds, each unmade and covered in stains, a grime-soiled desk, and a partially burnt office chair. It featured a dripping shower and a seat-less toilet, along with a buckled mirror which warped my head. To the exterior, the balcony was bedecked with bird-droppings, and the air conditioning unit had been stolen or otherwise misplaced. Here at least, I could enjoy superlative views of the smog-laden hottest city in Central Asia, while reading with alarm an incoming text from my new network provider: 'Welcome to Afghanistan...'

I made one bed to sit on, and placed my things on the other, not wanting to leave them on the sticky carpet. My faint hope of finding Wi-Fi was quickly disappointed, and my new phone network had not the signal strength for me to contact home. I wanted nothing more than to speak to Emma and my family; to let them know that I was OK, and of my predicament. I reckoned I could sneak past mullet lady, venture into Termez, and find Wi-Fi, yet my view from the balcony revealed roaming policemen on the streets. *One more day*, I told myself. One more day, and I'll be out of here. Don't risk more trouble. I'll comply, pay my fine, and be off.

There was a knock on my door at ten o'clock the next morning. I was quite happy to see Larina, and it seemed that she bore news. 'I have spoken to your lawyer. The court will accept an early fine of $500, and you'll be free to go today. Pack your bags, and let's go right now.'

I felt immediate relief, and hurried after Larina down the stairs. I gave a nod of good riddance to mullet lady and her pigsty hotel, then followed Larina into the waiting car of her colleague.

'How much cash do you have, Mr Oliver?'

'Around $60.'

'Then we need to visit the bank. We have until 12.00pm to make the payment – less than two hours – before the court closes for the weekend.'

We drove to the only bank in town to accept international bank cards, and there we found sheer chaos. Dozens of agitated locals packed the waiting room, jostling in queues or shouting for attention, stressed bank clerks dashed back and forth, papers in hand, telephones blared from every corner, workers typed and tapped while printers whirred. A sepia light filtered through the room from the antiquated lights above, and rare shafts of sun probed through the steel bars on the windows.

Larina led me to the security guard by the reception. 'We need to make a cash withdrawal for this tourist as soon as possible.'

'You need to get a ticket,' replied the guard. 'Go to that desk there,' he pointed, 'when your number is called, then you can see the bank clerk.'

'But this is a very urgent matter,' Larina replied.

'The tourist must wait like the locals.'

A long, tense hour passed until my number was called. I entered my travel card in the clerk's machine and requested $500. Nosey locals gathered uncomfortably close. I typed my pin, and then: *'Transaction failed.'*

I knew I had more than $500 in this account, but I was unsure of any daily limit. I tried again, this time requesting $450.

'Transaction failed.'

Now I was starting to get worried. If I failed to raise $500 cash by midday, I'd be going nowhere. I tried again for $400, then $350, then $300, when finally, my transaction was accepted. I had $360 in my hand, but it was not enough. Larina seemed as agitated as I did.

'I have another card, my British card,' I showed it to the bank clerk, but he shook his head.

'This card is not accepted here.'

'Is there anywhere in Termez where I can use this?'

'I'm sorry, sir, but no. You will have to come back on Monday.'

I retreated from the crowded bank with Larina, feeling dejected. I had forty minutes left to get the money, but what could I do? As we stepped back out onto the street, divine intervention revealed a gleaming black and yellow sign, which read: Western Union. One option remained.

'Larina, if I could make one phone call, I can possibly get the money before midday. Can I tether my phone to yours, and please use your internet?' It felt a bold question of an Uzbek border guard, but Larina nodded.

'Ok, you want to call your parents?'

'Yes, they might be able to send me the money.'

I got my phone online, and called my dad.

'Ol? Are you ok?' He sounded tired.

'Dad, I'm fine. I'm in Uzbekistan now, but I've had a problem at the border. They've told me that my co-codamol tablets are illegal, and I'm having to pay a fine. It's my only option. Unfortunately, though, I can't get enough money from my cards, so I wondered if you can transfer me some money via Western Union.'

He replied in true British fashion, 'It's 6.30 in morning. Flipping heck, Ol.'

I couldn't help but chuckle. 'I know, but I really need the money within half an hour, or I'll have to wait until Monday to be released.'

'I'll try and do it now.' I heard him shifting, then tapping on something. My mum was asking what was going on. 'Are you ok, though? You're not in jail or anything?'

'No, no, I'm staying in a hotel in Termez. It's very comfortable. They're looking after me. Dad, text me when it's done.

Can you send $200? And can you tell Emma, but make sure she isn't worried.'

'Alright, I'm working on it – shouldn't be long. Take care, and get in touch again as soon as you can.'

Larina let me keep hold of her phone, so that I would retain signal. Ten minutes later, a message came through: '*Money sent. X.*'

We dashed to the Western Union, and by 11.45am, I had $560 in my hand. My heart was racing; we'd done it; I was almost free.

Sharing my urgency and joy, Larina called my lawyer, 'We have the money, we're on our way to the…' but then her face sank. 'Oh,' she paused, 'I see. Ok.' Larina confronted me with a sigh. 'It's not possible.'

Not jail, I thought, *please not jail.*

'The court has not had time to review all your documents. I'm sorry, Mr Oliver, you will have to wait until Monday. We tried our best.'

With this, I returned sadly to the Pigsty hotel, greeted mullet lady, and climbed the stairs back to room 304. Larina told me that she was returning to the border this afternoon, and that somebody else would look after me now. 'An officer will bring you food this evening,' she said, 'good luck, Mr Oliver.'

I wallowed in my dungeon through the day, sometimes staring out at the street, or else flicking through the photos on my camera. I was soothed by the fact that my family were now in this with me, but nonetheless, I did not want it to endure. I knew of course that in relative terms to many, my plight was marginal, and it made me think back to my inspiring friend, Jawid. Jawid who endured three years of uncertainty as he travelled from Afghanistan to England, then ten years of confinement as he awaited asylum, missing his family all the while. Through each miniscule hour of my experience, my admiration for him grew, as did the value of freedom in my mind.

At seven o'clock, a limp fist struck my door. It was Ruslan, the toddler-shaped man, with a perverted penchant for English women. Ruslan wore his green suit and cap, and brought with him a serious-looking speechless fellow. They invited themselves into my room, Ruslan sitting on the bed opposite me, and his friend on the half-burnt chair just away from us, from where he watched.

'How are you, Oliver, my friend?' asked Ruslan.

'I'm OK, but I'm ready to leave this place.'

'Ah, but you're not free to go yet, are you? Monday. On Monday, you should be free. I will return your passport, and then you can go home to your family.'

'*Home?* I won't go home right away. I want to continue my journey through Uzbekistan.'

'But, why, Oliver? And How? You told the officers that you have very little money, that's why your fine is small,' he frowned. I glanced at his friend, whose face remained stern. Who was he? Secret Police perhaps? 'I think it would be wise for you to go home.'

I could not let Ruslan know I'd lied about money. Indeed, I did not trust him, and did not want him to know a thing about my future plans. 'Yes,' I replied, 'maybe I will go home.'

'Good, good,' Ruslan grinned, and his voice found a different tone. 'Tell me about your family. You have a nice family, yes?'

'Yes,' I nodded, watching Ruslan all the while. 'I have a very good family.'

'Come on, show me a picture of your family. You have a picture on your phone? We can talk like friends, Oliver. I am here to help you.'

I hesitated, but figured there would be little harm done. I scrolled through my pictures and found a recent holiday snap of myself, Emma, my mum and dad, and my brother and his girlfriend. I showed Ruslan, but with the light fingers of a practised pickpocket, he eased the phone out of my hand.

'Ah, yes, very nice, Oliver. You have a good family,' He started scrolling through my photos as he talked. Then, he passed my phone to his friend, who continued scrolling.

'Give it back.' The man ignored me.

'Why?' said Ruslan.

'Give it back!' I snatched my phone off the stern man, and glared at him for a second. My heart was beating more quickly, as I felt more and more uncomfortable in the presence of these two men. There was now a palpable tension in the room, and nobody spoke for ten long seconds.

'Relax,' said Ruslan, eyeing me, 'relax.' He leant back awkwardly, and looked towards my pockets, then returned, 'How much money do you have, Oliver?'

'Enough.'

'Show me, show me.'

I did not like where this was going. 'Why?'

'I want to see.'

'No,' I scowled, 'it's *my* money.'

'Oliver, *let me see.*'

'No!' In a swift move, I kicked Ruslan hard and square in the face. His body fell. He was out cold. His pal approached, fist reeled back, but I landed the first punch. I beat his head until he stopped moving. Ruslan was starting to stir. I grabbed my bags, pulled my passport from Ruslan's pocket, and left the room, locking them both inside.

I looked down at my hands, and wiped the blood on my t-shirt. What had I done? I couldn't think about that. I had to get out of here, fast. I bolted down the stairs and out through a side door. A flash of light marked my escape, and the evaporation of my daydream.

'Oliver,' said Ruslan, 'we are going now. I will leave this food for you.' He pointed to a plastic bag on my desk. 'I will come back tomorrow to check on you. Remember that you must not leave your room. This is very important. Do not leave your room.'

The two men stood, and finally withdrew from my bedroom. I locked and bolted the door behind them, then turned out my lights and went out onto the balcony. A minute later, I watched as they sauntered out of the hotel and along the moonlit street.

16

Whether Ruslan's threats were empty or not, I could not stay in here. I zipped up my jacket and crept out into the corridor. With no security cameras in sight, I continued down the stairwell and out through an open side-door, before skirting around the back of the hotel and out onto the streets.

A twilight chill removed the hot desert air, and the night sky was clear and fine. Fulsome trees overhead lent broad shadows to the pavement where I walked, mingling with money-changers, beggars and merchants. Beside me, a long row of shops included grocers, tea houses, eateries and a stuffy internet café. I stopped by a money-changer to trade some dollars for a clutch of Uzbek Som.

The national currency is peculiar in that the largest commonly available banknote, 500 Som, is worth just over ten pence. So changing just twenty dollars means receiving an inordinate stack of banknotes in return. I stuffed the cash in my bag, and continued to a nearby supermarket.

Ruslan had only left me some bread and two roasted chicken thighs, so I stocked up on food and bought myself a bottle of Uzbek beer. I plied the streets, glancing at my phone and hoping to find an open Wi-Fi network. Suddenly, one popped into range. I joined a group of like-minded youths outside the supermarket, and went online for the first time in days. It was a relief to speak with Emma and my parents. I assured them that I'd be released on Monday, and would be in touch again as soon as possible. Then, the police came into view.

There were four of them, standing across the car park, on the roadside. One officer stared. I sent a final text to Emma, then quick-stepped towards a large outdoor bazaar. There were books, spices, nuts, shoes and heaps of cotton; Uzbekistan's prime commodity. I darted through the stalls and re-emerged on the main street into a cluster of feisty money-changers.

They swarmed. 'Dollar? Som? Hey you, Americano? English? Hey!'

'Nyet. Nyet.'

I could see the policemen across the street now. They were chatting and walking in the direction of my hotel. Did they know about me? Were they looking for me? I hurried along my side of the street until I was a hundred yards ahead of them. Then, spying a gap through the traffic, I crossed the road and dashed into the grounds of my hotel, taking the same route around the back. I took a breath; confident I'd made it here unnoticed, yet my trouble was not over yet.

The side-door had been closed. I wrenched and twisted the handle, but to no avail. I cursed myself. I should never have left the hotel. My only route back into my room was via the insomniac mullet lady, ever watchful for fleet-footed foreigners. I walked around to the glass entrance, and saw mullet lady at once. She was sitting behind her desk in the empty reception area.

With audacity my only tool, I inflated my chest and strode through the doors. 'Salom!' I beamed.

Mullet lady replied with a confused and frowning nod.

On reaching room 304, I observed something from the balcony which I'd not expected to see. The four policemen emerged into view from the left. They continued gossiping as they patrolled the nearside of the street. They walked past the hotel entrance, past the car park, along the pavement, and out of sight, all without a glance at the Pigsty Hotel. What was I thinking? These men weren't watching me. They weren't following me, or chasing me.

I began to realise that Uzbekistan was having an unwelcome effect on me. I had lost all faith in the public figures one is taught to trust. I was left feeling a distinct sense of solitude and oppression, the cornerstones of paranoia. The sooner I could get out of this country, the better.

I remained in my room the next day, knowing that Ruslan's chubby knuckles could strike my door at any moment. I spent time updating my diary, and reading through a guidebook I'd bought for Central Asia. Today was Easter Sunday. I pictured my family gathered together, enjoying a morning walk, then an indulgent traditional dinner, laughing, playing games, drinking and being happy. I meanwhile could only pace my sticky carpet and chomp on stale bread. Finally, at 6pm, my plump tormentor returned. This time, he was alone.

'Come with me, Oliver. Let's go out for food together.'

I couldn't think of a less enticing prospect. 'I'm not very hungry. Thank you.'

'Ok, then maybe we can talk in your room for a while, like friends.'

This sounded even worse. 'Never mind. Let's go for food.'

Ruslan and I went downstairs, I tipped my head to mullet lady, and we ventured out into the evening.

'Did you leave the hotel since I last saw you, Oliver?' asked Ruslan. He walked uncomfortably close to my side, brushing his shoulder against mine with every step.

'No. I've just been reading in my room.'

'Are you sure?'

'Positive.'

'You must be looking forward to going home and seeing your family. Tomorrow, you can fly back to England.'

'I will fly back to England.'

My response made Ruslan smile. 'Ah, Oliver, we should keep in touch when you go back, and you can find an English girl for me. Send them to find Ruslan in Uzbekistan, and I will marry them! I want an English girl!'

What an honourable request. Having so fruitfully endeared himself to me, I would like nothing more than the pleasure of returning to my homeland, kidnapping some unfortunate woman, and sending her on a one-way trip to Uzbekistan to satisfy my maniacal, baby-faced pen-pal. 'No problem,' I replied, 'I will send the English girl to Ruslan.'

The buffoon beamed.

We arrived in the same fast food restaurant Larina and I had visited. Like before, it was packed with inquisitive students. Ruslan insisted on placing my order, before saying, 'It's 12,000 Som.'

'One moment.' I opened my bag.

'How much? How much have you got? Let me see.'

'Alright, you want to see my money?' A chance for revenge. I opened my wallet full of dollars to Ruslan, before spreading a wad of Uzbek Som before him. 'Look! Here's my money! Here's my money!' I thrust it towards him. Restless diners started chattering. Ruslan's face flashed red. For a pristinely-suited official straight out of training, publicly extorting a foreigner would be the height of indignity.

'Put it away,' he barked.

I shrugged. 'I thought you wanted to see my money.'

We returned to the hotel without another word, but I with a spring in my step. Ruslan told me to be ready at 9am tomorrow. It was time to get this thing over with.

The next morning, I was greeted with a scene from every respectable gangster movie. Ruslan (grumpy from last night), my interpreter and I entered my lawyer's tiny office. Laid out on the table was over 1.5 Million Uzbek Som, in 500 denomination banknotes. My lawyer had clearly worked up a sweat counting all these notes. She placed them in a large plastic bag, and traded them for my five one-hundred dollar bills.

'The paperwork is finished,' she said. 'We can travel to the court, and they will see us sometime today. Then, you will be free to go.'

Our destination lay in the dusty suburbs of Termez. We parked at the head of a guarded and barricaded road, which ran between two fields of barbed wire and desert-like scrub. Passing the soldiers, we continued along this road on foot, to reach a three-metre perimeter wall, marked only with a large set of solid steel gates, a single steel door, and a fortified window containing three watchful guards. It was an imposing place, whose interior remained unseen. A sign told me that this was a base of the infamous National Security Service, the Uzbek successor of the Soviet KGB.

Together, we entered a secure fenced area, outside of the main compound, and were told to wait on some steel benches by the guards. Five tedious hours passed and the high midday sun slowly cooked us from above. My lawyer spent most of this time inspecting her fingernails. Ruslan lay on a bench, looking dead. Meanwhile, my interpreter sought extensive employment advice from me, perhaps not realising I was a jobless vagabond.

At last, the steel door came open. Two soldiers invited us all in, except for Ruslan, whom we left to perish. We passed through a security check and into a broad courtyard, containing a patch of grass and some soldiers, and surrounded by brick walls, opaque windows, and nondescript doors. We were invited through one such door, where I was greeted with a desk full of papers, and a photograph of myself in the interrogators room at the border. A picture of the president, Islam Karimov, hung on the wall, but nothing else.

The two soldiers communicated something to my lawyer.

'They want your money, now,' said my interpreter, 'so they can start counting it.'

I handed one soldier the bag of money, and he disappeared out of the room.

'Now, just sign each of these documents, and the photographs.'

I followed the instructions, and within five minutes the soldier returned with a few thousand Som in change, before handing me that most treasured item, my passport.

My interpreter smiled. 'You are free to go.'

My shoulders lifted, and I felt a dark haze evaporate.

We retreated to the open air, which seemed crisper than before, and I loaded my shoulders with my bags.

'Ah,' said Ruslan, rubbing his eyes as he rose from the bench. 'So, it is finished, Oliver?'

'It's finished.'

'Very good. You can go home now.' He summoned my interpreter. 'Can you take him to the taxi rank. He needs to go to the airport right away.'

My interpreter agreed, and he and I split from the others.

'Don't forget my English girl!' called Ruslan, as he departed with my lawyer.

I was delighted to see the back of that oaf. My interpreter and I set towards the nearby taxi rank. 'Ignore him,' I said, 'I'm not going to the airport. I'm going to Boysun instead?'

'To Boysun?' he frowned. 'But why?

'For the mountains.'

My interpreter greeted the flat-caps and negotiated a keen price to Boysun on my behalf. I thanked him, and my shared taxi soon departed. With this, I rode out of Termez, passport in hand, and free once again. Despite my aching sense of injustice, I now felt a swell of liberation and even excitement at the prospect of exploring this country. However, If I believed my troubles in Uzbekistan were over, I was to be proved desperately wrong.

17

I had little clue where I was going. The mountain town of Boysun was given no mention in my guidebook, and was described online by only a few sparse web pages. These hinted at a mystical and enchanting land, isolated for centuries from greater Uzbekistan, whose unique rituals include goat fights, shamanism, horse races and dancing re-enactments of local folklore. Its lofty patch in the foothills of the Gissar Highlands promised my return to the mountains, and its lonely reputation implied a chance for me to elude the eye of the state.

We drove into the night, pausing often as vast goat herds crossed the highway. Sparse signs of modern civilisation showed. I saw mud-brick walls, old, weathered shepherds, and families eating around open fires. After three hours on the road, a few glimmering streetlights marked the approaching town centre. I paid and thanked my driver. He pointed to a nearby concrete building, before resting his head on his joined hands, as though asleep. I understood what he meant.

'Salom?' my voice echoed back to me. 'Salom! Hello!' Nothing. Wandering through the empty reception area, I came to a glazed door, behind which lay a dishevelled man sleeping on a couch. I knocked, and he exploded to his feet.

'Salom,' I said, smiling at him.

This was the only hotel in town, a lonesome stopover for traders, journeymen, and the like. The owner balled his fist and rubbed his eyes. We haggled a price for two nights. He gave me a key, and sent me along a dark and silent corridor.

My room was wallpapered in garish, smoke-stained colours, and the single bed was furnished with a thick hand-sewn blanket. There was only a thin net curtain covering the window, which I thought odd, but the room was ample for what I needed.

Having only snacked all day, I was eager for a wholesome meal before I ventured into the mountains tomorrow. Nearby, I found a basic supermarket, with a small café attached. As I shopped for food, I encountered three young men.

'Salom,' I said.

'Salom.'

'Do you speak English?'

'Yes, little,' said one boy, with large, bright eyes.

'Is there Wi-Fi or an internet café in Boysun? I need to contact my family.'

They looked at each other. 'Wi-Fi, Boysun, no. Internet café, no. Phone signal, no. Nothing.'

They seemed excited, and like they half-wanted to say something, but they just looked at me awkwardly, and then said goodbye. The fact that I'd been unable to contact home since Saturday evening was becoming a constant source of worry. Last my family knew, I was still detained. I did wonder if I'd made a mistake in coming to this eerie ghost town. Should I have travelled to a city instead, ignored my mountain goal in Uzbekistan, and brought relief to my family? Was I being foolish and selfish? I often considered that I was.

I ordered a giant plate of goulash in the cafe – beef stew, vegetables and potatoes – and sat near a group of charming old men. We enjoyed an amusing charade-based conversation about my journey, and my reason for visiting their town. They all wanted to shake my hand, to thank me for coming, and the café owner even said that my meal was a gift. Yet, just as Uzbekistan was showing its brighter side, two unwelcome figures entered.

I recognised their dark green uniform. The two officers, staring constantly, shared a word with the proprietor, before beckoning me outside.

Outside, the young men from the supermarket came to investigate. 'Problem, mister?'

'I don't know.'

'Passport,' said the officer.

I gave him my passport.

'Papers.'

I handed him the registration papers I'd collected from the Pigsty Hotel. My friend took the duty of interpreting for the officer, who had spent a while inspecting my documents. 'He ask, why, you, Boysun?'

'The mountains,' I replied, pointing in their direction.

'Where you stay?'

'The hotel, just here.'

The officer nodded. He was a short man with a straight back and jet black hair. For a few seconds, he simply surveyed me, as though committing to memory each aspect of my face. Then he muttered some closing words.

'He say, sorry. He just do job.'

I nodded, but I felt discontent.

When the officers had left us, my new pals invited me to a gathering at a local bar, owned by their family. The doors were locked when we arrived, but with a special knock, we were welcomed in. There I found a dozen young men, dealing cards, drinking beer and munching on Uzbek bread. Most of them were fiery boxers, with black eyes, bent noses and gold teeth, but they made me feel very welcome. We played cards and swigged beer.

After a while, my wide-eyed English-speaking friend, Zacchary, suggested we go to a clifftop viewpoint over the town. Seven of us squeezed into one car, and we raced through the village to reach a magnificent platform, beyond which the distant silhouetted mountains rose towards the milky-way. I became the on-request DJ, blasting British house music through the car speakers. Dancing, beer, cheering, laughter; this was my rebellion, my release-day riot. Down with the cops! The shackles of the law can't stop me!

Midnight approached with a haze, and a pair of headlights. The music stopped and everyone became sheepish.

'What's wrong?'

'It's the police,' said Zacchary.

A car braked hard beside us, and a towering policeman stepped out. He looked incredibly angry and he started ranting in Uzbek while waving his arms. The lads were rushing round, nodding like parrots and collecting beer bottles. Then, the colossus turned his attention to me.

'Passport and papers!'

I handed them to him.

'What are you doing here?'

'I was, I-.'

'Go back to Boysun, all of you. You, go back to your hotel, now!'

'OK, OK.' We piled into the car, and drove back to the town, with the police car tailing us most of the way. I said goodbye to the gang, and Zacchary invited me to another party the following night. I did not promise my attendance.

This unplanned evening of revelry had really been a bad idea. Not only was I back on the police radar, but my preparations for tomorrow's mountain climb were questionable. I downed a big glug of water, readied my pack, and bedded below my musky blanket.

Dawn broke with grey skies and the familiar crowing of a crooked taxi driver. He tried to drop me several miles from my destination, and at an exorbitant rate. I gave him half of what he asked for, and hitched a ride the rest of the way with a kind villager.

I was travelling up a mountain valley to the nearby shepherding community of Avlod, at 1450 metres. Here lay the trailhead towards a collection of craggy snow-capped peaks. At once, Avlod seemed more like the oasis I'd hoped to find. The village was split by a broad, sparkling river, which I crossed to begin my ascent. Chickens scuttled among the mud-brick houses. Ladies washed clothes in churning pools of water. Silver-bearded old men clasped their hearts and said 'Hello.' Young shepherds steered cattle through the pastures, while mule-riding farmers rode out towards the fruit trees. The sedate pace of life here slowed my very step, as the *real* people of Uzbekistan began recapturing my heart.

The climb itself was an unpleasant slog. The gradient was gentle, but the distance great. Underfoot, the terrain was either a thick and heavy clay, unstable scree, melting snow, or a horrible combination of the three. But the physical demands were superseded by a strange feeling. I was struggling to shake the sense of oppression brought upon my experiences over the last few days. Not helping was the sense that Boysun's officials were taking too great an interest in my presence. As such, and for the first time ever, the mountains brought no sense of freedom nor excitement.

Five hours later, I reached the summit of an unnamed 2800m peak with views of a darkening landscape. On my descent, four huge vultures circled overhead. I wondered if they'd come to put me out of my misery. Avlod reminded me to smile. A troop of ecstatic children followed me through the village, kicking a deflated football, and each shaking my hand. Their elation, despite the backdrop of their impoverished village, was truly heartwarming.

As I caught the hourly bus from Avlod to Boysun, I met a sincere man who looked like Cristiano Ronaldo's diminutive Uzbek cousin. Seeing that I was tired and dirty, he invited me back to his house for dinner. My inclination was to decline. I wanted to hole-up in my bedroom until the morning and merely dodge any watchful eyes. Yet Ronaldo persevered, and I agreed.

My subsequent time with him was further proof that humans need not share a common language to have a conversation, or to enjoy each other's company. Ronaldo did not know a word of English, but I soon learned that he was an electrician, who maintained the local power grid. He was also a keen photographer, and each year, he took the class photos for the nearby school.

Ronaldo led me to his family's idyllic plot by a tributary of the main river. He had two cows, some fruit trees, and a diverse vegetable patch. His house was larger than most, and he was proud to reveal that he had built most of it himself. As the evening went by, an unexpected emotion took hold. Ronaldo's two young children were smiling and playful. His wife was charming and polite. He had a good home, with views of the mountains, and a bountiful orchard to sustain his family. Ronaldo was content and carefree. He had reached the exact thing that had sent me on my journey, *self-actualisation*, the achievement of one's full potential. And he had done so in his very own home. I felt envious. Today was proof that the mountains cannot be a constant source of happiness. Maybe I've had it wrong all this time. Perhaps paradise is not a place, but rather an elusive state of mind. Right now I craved not the mountains, but my childhood sweetheart, Emma, and our future home, and our wedding. With this expedition, had I chosen fleeting thrills over lasting joy, or had it merely taken this journey to make me realise that?

I left Ronaldo's house like so, feeling pensive. His wife had cooked a fabulous feast of several courses, and had even given me a traditional Boysun skullcap as an eternal gift. I was humbled with gratitude. As I meandered through the sundown darkness, Uzbekistan's disparity between people and state reignited in the timeliest fashion.

Boysun was a place of day. By night, all fell quickly silent. No cars plied the road, and few locals walked the streets. So, I was alone when I reached my hotel after a long trek through the village. A line of trees cast myself and the pavement in shadow. Ahead, there was an open gate, a path through a small garden, then the hotel. Two parking spots sat to the left, one of which was occupied, at that moment, by a police car. The short policeman from last night got out.

I froze.

He walked slowly, but deliberately, across the front of the hotel, past the hotel entrance, and to the fourth window of the ground floor, where he furtively halted. No lights were on in this room, for it was mine, and I was stood watching the scene. The officer held his hand to my window and peered through. What should I do? Do I shout, or remain hidden?

I did not move, nor speak a word. Ten seconds passed, then the police officer moseyed back past the hotel, and climbed into his car. I simply could not believe what I had seen. However ineptly, I was being spied upon! I could have been sat in my room, with that creep peering through my window. What the hell did the police want from me?

As his car pulled back onto the main road, I darted across the garden, through the entrance, along the corridor, and into my bedroom. I left the lights turned off, and then draped my bed sheet across the window to add opacity to the thin net curtain.

I enjoyed scant rest through the night, bag propped against the bolted door, ears and eyes keen for noise or movement outside. The next morning, I was gone before dawn.

18

The ancient city of Bukhara lay over two-hundred miles away. At daybreak, I found myself travelling west across the desert, in the passenger seat of an old Russian Lada. Beside me, one of Boysun's flat-caps, and the only man to see me leave the secluded village by the mountains.

I journeyed through the day, changing taxis in every major town. Each passing mile quelled the residual distrust in my mind. Extraordinary rain obscured Bukhara at dusk. This, a millennia-old city of minarets, mausoleums, madrasahs and ramparts. Exotic sculptures of stone and tile showed through the haze. Then, the scent of musky drizzle drifted. I walked alone through the downpour, enchanted at once by this new domain; a living collage of the past. Courtyard doors lay ajar in the backstreets, bringing glimpses of kiln-tending cooks and open-mouthed children, fingers in the raindrops.

I arched my head towards the sky and kneaded my dripping hair. The rain poured down my skin like glugs of warm oil, cleansing my body. I felt anonymous, lonesome and free. I navigated to a steel door on the edge of the old city, where I was greeted, with the ring of a bell, by a compassionate face.

'Oh! No, no, no, no.' said the lady, tutting, and shaking her head with sympathy. She placed a hand on my shoulder and led me across the courtyard towards the front door of her hostel.

I gave a broad smile in return. I might have been drenched but I was the happiest I'd been since I arrived in Uzbekistan.

'Do you have a room for the night?' I asked.

'Yes,' said the lady, 'but, me – erm – English, no. Daughter, English, yes. She, hostel, later.'

The lady gave me a warm towel and showed me to a dorm room. I was the only guest there. She flicked on the water heater for the shower, and left me in my puddle. The prospect of a hot shower was not the cause of my delight though. I dropped my bags, logged onto the Wi-Fi on my phone, and called Emma.

I heard a single ring, and then a flood of tears.

'I'm ok, Emma. I'm ok.' A lump was swelling in my throat.

'We didn't know if you were in prison, or if you'd gone to the mountains and had an accident, or if you were missing, or if you were, were -.'

It was intense; the panting sound of relief, of concern, of undivided love. My four days of silence had sent Emma on a precipitous tightrope, and with this phone call, she had stepped across the chasm of uncertainty.

'We didn't know what to do, or who we could call for help. We didn't know where you were. I couldn't sleep last night with worry. Please, Oli, please don't do this to us again. It's too much. I just want you home.'

And I wanted to be home. There's an airport in Bukhara. I could fly home the next day. Sure, people would know that I've failed to complete my trip, but the embarrassment of that wouldn't last long. I'd be back with Emma. We could start to decorate our house together, and make final plans for the wedding. Then, I could earn a bit of money doing something. I could get a job, and all would be just fine! But, *what kind of job?* Who would pay me to talk about my trip if I didn't make it to the end? Who would publish a book about an unfinished journey? Who would have faith in a mountain leader who *himself* is unable to persevere? This expedition was a unique moment in my life. Do I ride the tough times, and take a stab at leading a life of mountains and adventure, or do I give in, and return to the day job?

'I'm coming home, Emma, but not quite yet. My Turkmen visa is due to arrive tomorrow. I have five days to cross Turkmenistan, then I'll reach Azerbaijan, and the final leg of my journey. I've paid my fine, I've bagged my Uzbek mountain, and I'm hungry to continue towards Istanbul.'

After a long breath, Emma replied, unwavering in devotion. 'I believe in you, Oli.'

A long, steaming shower soothed my body. When the rain subsided, I enjoyed a plate of shashlik by an ancient Silk Road bazaar, and plotted my final move across Central Asia.

Turkmenistan lies due south, a vast and sandy barrier between here and Iran. It is known in travelling circles as the North Korea of Central Asia. Turkmenistan's outlandish autocrats have built huge structures of marble and gold, declared themselves 'Eternal Leaders', encouraged their people to chew bones to keep their teeth strong, and syphoned billions of dollars into their gilded wallets. From the seldom travellers who had journeyed there, I had heard tales of spying secret policemen, hotel room searches, bugging, and internet surveillance. I was somehow attracted to visit this bizarre totalitarian republic, but I had the distinct sense that to do so would be to step deeper into the lion's den.

My target was Turkmenbashi, a port eight-hundred miles away, across the Karakum Desert, on the coast of the Caspian Sea. From there, unscheduled cargo ferries ply the oil-rich waters towards Azerbaijan. If I could make it there, this is where my overland journey would resume. But, there was a problem. The unique code for my date-specific, five-day Turkmen visa was yet to arrive, following my embassy visit in Dushanbe. If I did not receive the code and enter Turkmenistan within the next 36 hours, my tentative plan would crumble; my escape from Uzbekistan foiled.

For now, though, I sipped on green tea and admired the nearby fountains and madrasahs. Beside me, scholarly men debated some important issue, smoke coiled from oily vats of plov, and those elusive creatures, foreign tourists, wandered occasionally past. Bukhara was a longtime favorite of adventurous, golden-pound spending globetrotters, and the next morning, with still no sign of my visa code, I decided to find out why.

I had contacted a friend from the hostel in Dushanbe, who promised to chase the Turkmen Embassy on my behalf. For now, though, all I could do was wait. Bukhara is a true and remarkable wonder. To wander here is to wander through the ages. The 5th century Ark fortress is the city's oldest structure. It stands surrounded by huge bulging ramparts, like the buttresses of an ancient oak; twenty metres high and topped by pointed chunks of stone. This was once the palace for the Emirate of Bukhara. In 1839, a fellow Briton arrived here as I did. He was an emissary named Colonel Stoddart, sent to reassure the incumbent Emir that Britain's Afghan invasion would not encroach Bukhara's territory.

Stoddart thrice insulted the barbaric Emir, first by ignoring custom and riding a horse to the gates of the fortress, then by not delivering a letter from Queen Victoria, and finally by having the audacity of arriving without a gift for his regal host. Stoddart was tossed in a pit. Three years passed, a hapless would-be rescuer, Captain Conolly, joined Stoddart in prison. The pair were marched outside the fortress, made to dig their own graves, and beheaded by sword before the watching Emir. Maybe my own arrival in this country was not so bad after all.

Nearby, dominating the cityscape, stands the breathtaking

Kalon Minaret. Almost fifty metres high and nine-hundred years old, this structure is of such ornate beauty that even Ghengis Khan supposedly ordered his rampaging troops to leave the minaret intact. I explored opulent mosques, lively old bazaars and traditional tearooms. No place on my journey yet has evoked such intense visions of the Silk Road as Bukhara, which did so through each of my five overawed senses. Wasted time meant I had missed the chance to visit Uzbekistan's other fantastical cities, of Samarkand, Khiva and Kokand, but I was glad that my uncertain road had delivered me to this particular gem in the sprawling desert.

That evening, I received word from my contact in Dushanbe that my Turkmen visa had been approved, and my unique code sent to the nearby border. I had lost one day of my visa, leaving me with just four days to journey through Turkmenistan, and hope to find a ferry across the Caspian Sea.

Being the only guest at my hostel, the owners invited me to join their family dinner that evening. We consumed the Uzbek delicacy, Plov. Mekhrangiz, the English-speaking daughter, and I, enjoyed a candid and fascinating discussion about her life in Uzbekistan. She liked living in Bukhara, and had undergone a high-level of education. Her main vexation though was the occasional feeling that she was trapped. She hoped one day to study or work abroad. In Russia, perhaps, or Europe. But Mekhrangiz explained that it's very hard for young, unmarried Uzbek women to travel overseas. Permission must be granted first by her parents, and then, more difficultly, by the state. Mekhrangiz would scarcely stray from *safer* topics of conversation, and I wondered if she held beliefs she wished not to share with a relative stranger like me. Curiously, though, near the time of writing, Mekhrangiz reached St. Petersburg, and there got married quickly. Whether or not she intends to return to her homeland, I am not sure.

I left the hostel the next morning, rucksacks on shoulders, ready to attend to an important errand. Turkmenistan is a mainly cash-based society. It is said to be difficult, if not impossible, to withdraw cash using international bank cards. Moreover, I had a $50 visa fee to pay at the border. With $30 left in my wallet, I desperately needed money.

'Sorry,' said the clerk of a nearby bank, 'first day of the month. No withdrawals today. Wait until Monday [three days away].'

I visited another bank, and heard the same story. Then another, and another. I was turned away from six separate banks over the course of two hours walking around the city. I tried every ATM I could find, but they were each empty of cash. I needed to get moving fast, but without a pocketful of dollars, my plan was faltering.

By midday, I came to realise that it would be impossible for me to continue into Turkmenistan. Adding further complication, I had 36 hours to leave Uzbekistan, but could not enter Azerbaijan until a day after that. I could not return to Tajikistan, and it would be futile to travel east to Kyrgyzstan. I had $30 and 36 hours to leave Uzbekistan, and my only option was to journey north.

Kazakhstan has one Caspian Sea port, linked with Azerbaijan, named Aktau. Yet the cargo ships are said to depart only every ten or fourteen days, and getting to Aktau would mean travelling 1500 miles across deserted Kazakh steppe. I decided to swallow some pride, and book a flight from Shymkent, Kazakhstan, to Baku, where I could finally embark on my final leg, and most importantly, make my return to the mountains.

That night, I found myself on a sleeper train from Bukhara to the capital, Tashkent. I shared a cabin with an odd cross-eyed businessman, who liked sitting on the edge of his bed and staring at me. For fourteen hours, I lazed a yard away from this fellow, in our snug wooden cabin, considering by what means I'd defend myself when he decided to attack. I reckoned if I hurled him out the window, along with all his possessions, nobody else would even know. They do it all the time in the movies.

With luck, his attack never came, and I reached a bland corner of Tashkent unscathed. The city imparted a trio of police passport checks on me, as a welcome gift, before punting me towards the border in a smelly shared taxi. This border post was much larger and busier than the other. With some basic luggage checks, some final declarations, and a merciful stamp in my passport, I bade farewell to my great Central Asian adversary. I may have paid my debt to the state, but I really owed it to the people; to those who, through humbling acts of kindness, had injected the special moments of delight so sought when travelling through the backwaters of the world. I cannot pretend, though, that I'll be rushing back.

Then, facing horizons new, I looked down at the four

wrinkled dollars in my hand. I showed them, along with a remorseful face, to a young flat-cap in training. He agreed to take me to Shymkent. It was a humdrum but likable city. I withdrew a modest bounty from a cash machine, and scurried straight into a local diner.

That evening, I was keen for a decent night's sleep after a long journey, so I was delighted to find a modern-looking guesthouse, with a tinted glass-front, at an incredibly reasonable rate. Something did seem off though. I shortly judged, by the lewd sounds coming from the room next door, and the stream of sheepish men in the reception area, that I was almost certainly frequenting a brothel.

So it was, my final night in Central Asia. I lay among a night-long chorus of banging headboards and the pungent smell of sweat, near penniless, in a city five-hundred miles from my predetermined trail, wondering how it had come to this.

19

If Asia is a dormant beast, lying motionless in the deep oceans of the world, then the curving chain of peaks from Hong Kong to Istanbul are its mountainous spine. Each summit holds its own tale, whether carved by bludgeoning ice, or upraised by lava, overrun by impregnable jungle, or condemned by the bombs of man. For almost ninety days, these mountains have been my way-points, thrusting me westward across the continent. Now though, it seemed, the mountains had gone missing.

Where Asia's peaks swung south through the rugged ranges of Afghanistan and Iran, the human geopolitical invention had turned me away. Like a stone hurled from a summit, I had tumbled downwards, beyond even the valleys below, and onto the distant plateaued shoulder of the dormant beast. So I found myself on the great Kazakh steppe; an expansive grassland which stretches from here to Moscow and beyond. My goal now was to return to the jagged terrain that I so savour.

I raced through the skies, stopping at Almaty, then Astana, the Kazakh capital, before turning west once again towards Baku, and Azerbaijan. This would be my gateway into the Caucasus region, a volatile land of ex-soviet countries and recent war. The Caucasus mountain range is a perfect ridge in beast's spine, rising from waters of the Caspian, then sloping, seven-hundred miles away, back into the Black Sea. The pinnacles here soar above five-thousand metres, and happen to reside in an altogether new and enchanting place.

Recent days brought news of violent fighting in Nagorno-Karabakh, a self-administered region, disputed between Armenia and Azerbaijan for the last thirty years. Dozens, possibly hundreds, of soldiers were reported to have been killed along the border, and many predicted the resurgence of full-scale war between two of the planet's most acrimonious enemies.

I disembarked at Baku's Heydar Aliyev Airport, named after Azerbaijan's former president and member of the country's ruling family. The airport is a dazzling, modern architectural masterpiece, of an opulence rarely seen outside the rich cities of the Arabian Gulf. A line of attractive female border guards whisked me through customs without a hitch, and I was soon trundling towards the capital at midnight.

Azerbaijan pitches itself as *The Land of Fire*. It is home to mud volcanoes and burning mountains, each startling indicators of the country's bountiful oil and gas reserves. Indeed, it is the wealthiest country in this region, and lavish spending in Baku is said to have created a mesmerizing city. As I cruised along, chattering flat-caps in the front seats, I witnessed divine geometric sculptures beside majestic buildings of stone, each illuminated like paintings on a gallery wall. I arrived in the characterful backstreets, and climbed the twisting staircase of Baku's only hostel.

It seemed I'd been blessed with some rare fortune as I was sent not to a dorm room, but to my very own luxurious twin room. Yet, after returning from a shower, I found that my fortune was not so. In the bed beside my own, snoozing like a sloth, lay an eighty-year-old Japanese woman. A more awkward night's sleep, I have never endured.

I spent the following day exploring the city. I found it to be immaculate, attractive and well-manicured, if a little quiet. There were people around, but they barely raised their voices. Even a cluster of flag-waving youths reacting to the skirmish with Armenia did so with hardly a noise. I understood that the Azeri character was one of modesty, politeness and privacy. I had read, even, that Azeri people do not like to smile at strangers, reserving this gesture for only close friends and family. One-poorly translated website went as far as declaring that if you smile at an Azeri person, 'they may think you are mentally-handicapped.' So I kept my smile to myself, and noticed that the locals did the same.

Finding this custom unusual, if intriguing, I set myself the challenge of breaking through the impassive shell of an Azeri native, and discovering the true character that lies beneath.

My exploration of Baku took me along old cobbled laneways, where wrinkled traders displayed a trove of antiques: brass sculptures and lamps, lanterns and candlesticks, carpets and treasure chests, pewter bowls and traditional skullcaps. Then I wandered through elegant gardens to the 15th century Palace of the Sharvanshahs, a multi-story maze of ornate stone and the former domain of a long-since vanquished kingdom. From here, one can spy south to the famous Flame Towers, three recently built skyscrapers akin to sharks fins rising from the city. Gaze east, and one can view the five-hundred-year-old Maiden Tower. According to legend, a cruel king locked his young maiden in this tower to hide her from her lover. The lover killed the king and came to rescue the maiden, but on hearing footsteps in the tower, and assuming it was the king, the maiden leapt from the rooftop and splatted on the ground.

Baku holds a mystic charm. The streets seem to whisper of an untold and mythical past. More so, its residents, unspeaking but watchful, look as though a grand secret is theirs to retain. For the single day I dwelt here, the city enraptured my imagination.

That evening, I came to face my elderly roommate over a cup of tea at the hostel.

'My name is Aiko.' She was short and smiling, with a youthful face.

I told her about my journey, and that I was looking for a mountain to climb in Azerbaijan.

'Oh,' she replied, 'but the mountains now are dangerous. I was recently in Kazbegi, Georgia.'

'Beneath Mount Kazbek?'

'Yes, and every day and through the night we heard rock fall and avalanches; *whoosh*,' she splayed her fingers.

I knew that there had been heavy snow in the mountains over recent days, and that the country was currently gripped by unseasonable heat, making for hazardous conditions.

'But the mountains are beautiful too, aren't they?' She asked.

'They certainly are. Were you – *are you* – a mountain climber too?'

She showed a twinkle in her eye. 'I too have visited many countries and climbed many mountains. Now though, it is time for young people like you to go and climb the mountains. Take care.' She shook my hand and left.

My research had centered on an obscure village in the valleys of the southern Caucasus, named Laza. From here, a jagged expanse of mountains radiate northwards, increasing in height towards the Russian border. I could access Laza via the larger town of Qabala, which I set towards the following day.

It seemed that the flat-cap phenomenon had extended into these western reaches of the ancient Silk Road. The taxi drivers here were even more distinctive than their Central Asian counterparts, with leather caps, leather jackets, leather shoes, dark sweaters and dark jeans. As I approached a boisterous crowd of flat-caps, they each frowned at the trainers I wore, until I began proceedings with a single word:

'Qabala.'

'Qabala, Qabala!' they cried. I was instantly mobbed. One old fellow with three teeth grabbed my shoulder, while a young lad with scars latched onto my opposite arm. They each shouted, 'Qabala, Qabala!' while the crowd jostled. I was a rag-doll between pit bulls. Fighting against the young lad, I asked, 'How much?'

'Fifty manat!'

'Twenty.'

'Twenty!' his eyeballs popped out and he spat on the floor.

I turned to Three-Teeth on my shoulder. 'Twenty manat?'

He frowned.

I showed him a twenty manat note. Before he could respond though, the young scoundrel shoved him in the chest. He shouted something like 'The bearded bastard is mine!'

While the crowd tried to pacify him, I turned to the old fellow, and flashed him the banknote, 'Qabala: twenty manat?'

'Da, Ok.' He nodded, and we stole away.

Three-Teeth's nearby car looked as old as its driver. The tyres were haggard and crusted layers of rust encircled each panel of bodywork. As we got in, the seats were covered in assorted fabric to conceal the springs below. I thought I'd haggled a bargain until now. Three-Teeth gave the pedals a kick, twisted the key, and the engine spluttered into life.

So, we began our long journey into the mountains. As the flat-caps do, Three-Teeth occasionally collected other passengers from the roadside, and dropped them at various points along the way. He seemed curious about me. He tried to converse in Azeri, then Russian, but neither were any use. We shared no more than a couple of common words. Thus, he just stared, considering who I might be.

Outside of Baku, any sign of wealth quickly vanished. We passed through simple towns and villages and along dusty roads. At midday, Three-Teeth pulled into a rugged roadside diner for some lunch. We sat opposite one another in a seat by the window, and my driver ordered food on my behalf. A handful of other journeymen lazed around, drinking tea and prattling.

We waited for a time, Three-Teeth maintaining his curious eye, until our food was delivered. First, bread, then wild salad leaves, then two bowls of meaty objects in a deep sauce of oil and garlic. I had no clue what they were, but could only guess, based on their oval shape, size and appearance, that they were the testicles of some poor castrated beast.

As Three-Teeth began to eat, he asked our young waiter if he spoke English.

'Yes,' said the boy, 'little.'

Three-Teeth's eyes lit up. Using his translator, he asked me what I was doing here, and where I had come from.

'I'm from England, and for the last three months I have been travelling across Asia from Hong Kong, towards Istanbul.'

The boy interpreted my reply.

Three-Teeth did a half laugh, half cough. And again. And again. Was he choking on a testicle? He convulsed again, then erupted into outright laughter. 'Three months!' he replied. 'You have taken three months to travel all across Asia, and reach Azerbaijan? Don't you know about aeroplanes? It would have taken you less than a day!'

He retold my tale to all the other customers, tears in his eyes, '*Three months!*' and they all joined in with laughter. I too was laughing. In the simplest terms, and in the age of transcontinental flights, my journey *was* quite absurd. With this, as Three-Teeth continued to howl, and his flat-cap chums chuckled, I felt not derision, but instead the warm and welcoming embrace of Azerbaijan.

I grimaced through my bowl of testicles. Then, Three-Teeth and I, friends anew, were on our way again. His old car was starting to whimper, and as we reached Qabala after four hours on the road, it emitted some feeble coughs. Three-Teeth beat on the dashboard, and cursed. Meanwhile, my directions got lost in translation as Three-Teeth pulled through the gates of a spectacular five-star resort hotel. His spluttering vehicle drew grimaces from the watching concierge.

'No, no,' I said, 'not here.'

Three-Teeth asserted that it *was* here, and as he pulled in front of the grand hotel doors, his wheezing little motor choked and died. Three-Teeth slammed the steering wheel. With great indignity, we climbed out onto the forecourt.

'Good afternoon, Sir,' said the approaching concierge. 'Do you, erm, have a reservation?' He squinted at Three-Teeth, who was poking around the grimy engine-block.

'No. We came here by mistake. I'm staying somewhere else.'

'Well, excuse me, but could you please move your car? We have many guests arriving soon.'

Oil was seeping onto the polished marble entrance. Three-Teeth kicked his car and grumbled, hands covered in grease.

Just then, a regally-dressed Arab gentleman approached from the reception.

'Hello!' he beamed, 'do you have a problem with your car?'

'I'm afraid so.' We shook hands.

'Please let me help you,' he bowed. He swept round to the front of the car, pristine white silks floating behind him. Hands crossed behind his back and stomach poking forward, he pried under the bonnet. I joined him, and pretended to be less clueless than I actually was. The car was in a shocking state of disrepair, fixed with tape, partially replaced with plastic bottles, and held together with rope.

'Where are you from?' I asked of the Arab.

'I am from Saudi...' he smiled, before bending towards the engine, 'originally. I have lived in England, like you, for the last ten years.' He edged past Three-Teeth, and began meddling with pipes and wires. 'And I am in the business of oil. My occupation takes me all around the world, and I'm here in Azerbaijan for a conference. Are you attending the conference too?'

'*No.*'

'Ah, but you are staying in this hotel? It is very cheap really. So much cheaper than those in London.'

'Oh, no,' I scratched my head, 'I'm staying at-, at another hotel.'

'Well, let me help you get there.' He beckoned Three-Teeth to start the ignition, as he clutched some wires. With a jolt and a puff, the engine started, and the Arab clapped his hands. The sleeves of his spotless robes were now tarnished. 'Don't worry about these,' he caught me looking, 'I'm happy to assist a traveller in need.'

I looked across at the concierge, who was dumbfounded like I, before thanking the Arab, and rejoining Three-Teeth. A short journey across Qabala delivered me to a much more modest abode. I paid my dues, and bade farewell to my vacant-mouthed chum.

The mountains finally beckoned.

At dawn the next day, I hitchhiked towards the village of Laza. We rode through a wide and steepening valley, split by a cloudy river, and surrounded by alpine peaks. Not famed for mountaineering, this region has no trails, and therefore no trailheads. I left the driver at a bend in the road at 1300 metres. Beyond, the sounds of a stirring village could be heard, of cockerels and cattle, muttering and movement. It seemed from a distance a tiny rural place, absent of all Baku's riches. But today was not about the village, nor its people. I would remain alone; just myself and my pilgrimage to the mountains.

The skies were bright and clear, with the occasional fluffy cloud spiraling the tops. I first crossed a grazing pasture, reaching it before the cows. Then, began my ascent through a steep forest of walnut trees and colourful shrubs. I climbed roots and creepers to reach a broad ridge blanketed by fresh snow. The air was crisp, energising my steps. I bypassed the tree line, and a hot sunbeam fell across my path. Grey replaced green; boulders for bushes. The ground steepened. The ridge narrowed.

I probed through broken terrain for an hour to reach a snow-white crest. The powder here was more than a metre deep, long since softened by the sun. To my right, a sub-peak at 2250 metres. To my left, a long ridge then the ominous bulging form of my destined mountain, rising to 2800 metres. I glanced right, and turned left. The ridge became my guide, my illumined path through the highlands. My footsteps broke its undulating spine as I trekked on.

From my lofty vantage, the anthem of the mountains became more distinct, with echoing rock fall and avalanches all around. Senses heightened, I paused to survey the pinnacle ahead. Approaching from the east, I could see that the southern aspect was a near-vertical cliff. The north face was plastered with extremely deep snow and looked prone among the hot conditions on the mountain. Directly ahead, poking through the snow, was what looked like an intermittent line of boulders. They stretched towards the summit, along the apex of the southern cliff.

As I plotted my next move, two things happened. First, a thundering rock fall from the nearest valley. Then, having gathered in the north, a dense mass of clouds swept across the ridge, causing a temporary white-out. I decided to go on and attack the mountain directly, keeping to the boulders where possible.

They weren't boulders. They were giant lumps of saturated mud, interspersed with razor-sharp slate-like rocks. I climbed over these, and through the steepening snow in between, until I reached a dangerous crux.

To my right and above was a swollen melting cornice. To my left and below was a sheer drop into the fog. I took a couple of steps, then the ground beneath my feet collapsed, tumbling down the cliff with snow and rocks. Shot with adrenaline, I latched onto a rock with a vice like grip. It wobbled in the mud. If it gave, I would fall.

20

Delicately, heart pounding, I heaved myself onto a small ledge and kicked my crampons into the sludge-like snow. I didn't realise for a minute, but the sharp rock which had saved me, had almost sliced the top of my finger off. Globules of blood stained the snow around my feet.

I waited there until the cloud cleared. The area I had just climbed was much steeper than I'd thought. I looked down at the trail of fallen mud and rocks way below. I turned back, but the descent was difficult and uncertain, neither the snow nor the mud being remotely stable.

I eventually ran back onto the ridge to cross towards the smaller peak at 2250 metres. As I did so, an absurd phenomenon took hold. From adrenaline came energy. From doubt: assurance. From fear: euphoria. I charged onto the summit, elation coursing through my veins. Dull clouds cleared to blue sky and I raised my arms to the vacant mountain range. Where else in life could I find such excitement, such risk, such magnificence? I admired the beauty of danger. Nothing besides has such life-giving force. I leant my hailing voice to the anthem of the mountains, and realised once again why to flog kitchens was to waste my sole existence.

The Land of Fire had reignited my mountain quest. Now, three more countries and three more challenges lay between myself and the edge of Asia: Istanbul and the end of my journey. After spending a second night in Qabala, I resumed my trail to the west. In the last couple of days, the fighting between Azerbaijan and Armenia had ended in ceasefire. News of the allayed turmoil boded well. Armenia was my next destination.

It is impossible for anybody to cross the militarised border of these two nations, so my journey to Armenia would pass through Georgia and take two days. I *could* beeline for Turkey directly through Georgia, but knowing that Armenia is a land of snowcapped volcanoes, I felt it was worth the detour.

'I will take you, my friend. Yes, yes, come with me!' A thickset young flat-cap greeted me in the Azeri border town of Balakan.

'Ok,' I replied, 'but I only have four manat.'

He hesitated, having already latched onto my rucksack. I saw scars on his knuckles. 'But the price is ten.'

'Can you take me for four or not?' This was no charade. I was empty-pocketed once more.

He smirked, disbelieving, and looking me up and down. 'Ok.'

I got into his car, and it was a mistake.

The border lay only fifteen minutes away, but once we cruised out of the town and onto an empty tree-lined road, Knuckles looked at me. 'You have more money, yes?'

'No,' I shrugged. 'four manat. Nothing else.' I showed him the notes.

He shook his head, squeezed his steering wheel, then he tore one hand free, and jabbed a pointing finger at me. 'You have more money. I know, I know,' he tapped his skull.

'*I have four manat.*'

Seething, Knuckles stamped on his accelerator and started to swerve left and right across the road. He was twitching with anger. He turned up the volume of his Azeri dance music and began shouting along to it. This guy was a maniac.

The Caucasus, in parts, harbours some of the world's most fearsome mafia, terrorists, and militia. Many of its male inhabitants are well accustomed to violence. I, off the rugby fields of my Wigan youth, am not so. I braced. What kind of man was I sharing a car with?

'Empty your pockets!' He slammed the brakes.

I did so. 'Look, I have nothing.'

'Your back pockets.'

I showed him those too. 'Nothing!'

He switched back to the accelerator and blasted the music even louder. My eyes flashed between him and the road. He was a fearsome, swelling, rancorous beast, on the knife-edge of sanity.

'Take me to the border,' I demanded. 'We agreed on four manat. If I had more money, I would give it to you.'

He kept on swerving and shouting. I remained tense. Would he veer into the forest and butcher me? Would he call his mafia pals and take me hostage? Would he hurl me onto the roadside and steal my bags?

With relief, the border post came into view. Knuckles slammed on, nearly sending my head through the windscreen, which made him smile. I tossed him my last pennies, grabbed my bags and bolted out of Azerbaijan.

The crossing was swift and smooth. One inebriated backpacker in Bishkek had sworn that the friendly Georgian border guards would give me a bottle of wine as a welcome gift. This was sadly not the case, but the greeting was warm. I withdrew a wedge of Georgian Lari, and bargained a price to the capital, Tbilisi, arriving there in the early evening.

The differences between here and Azerbaijan were subtle at first. Gone were the central village minarets, replaced by robust churches. Billboards and signs were now adorned with the most handsome, delicate script, like a fictional tongue from *The Lord of the Rings*. The outskirts of Tbilisi felt like Eastern Europe, while the ancient cobbled laneways in the centre could be the canal-side boulevards of Amsterdam. There was a hip and edgy feel to the city. Scruffy artists mingled with slick young professionals and wealthy, wine-sipping ladies. Most notably though, none of them gave me the slightest flicker of attention. I almost felt like I blended in.

The ancient Kingdom of Iberia (now Georgia) embraced Christianity in the 4th century. Yet, occupying precarious territory, Georgia was for centuries caught between the feuding empires of Rome and Persia. Then, it was overrun through the ages by Mongols and Ottomans. The Soviet Empire was the last to reign here, before Georgia's recent independence in 1991.

Peace, however, was slow to follow. Since liberation, Georgia has endured a coup d'état, a fierce civil war, a revolution and a war with Russia, along with earthquakes and floods. The latter occurred in Tbilisi in 2015 and famously ended with escaped zoo animals roaming the city. A tiger mauled some poor fellow to death, a hippo chomped on street-side trees, and a runaway penguin was collected sixty miles downriver.

I was charmed at once by the city. With the mountains calling though, I made south for Yerevan, the Armenian capital, the next morning.

The border guard tapped twice on his desk. 'Passport.' He was clean shaven, with a square chin. The scent of cheap aftershave wafted from his booth.

He inspected my face against my photograph, then thumbed through the pages of my passport. He arrived at a pair of black stamps and his jaw went tight.

'*Azerbaijan?*' He scowled.

'Yes,' I replied, 'but I'm just a tourist. Is there a problem?'

His face was so tightly knotted with disgust that he only nodded, and muttered something into his radio. I was ushered away, and shortly approached by a more senior officer.

'Come with me.'

He led me to a separate booth in full view of the queuing onlookers. Keeping his lips pursed, this fleshy officer retrieved a pen from his shirt pocket, a notepad from his jacket pocket, and the glasses from the top of his forehead. A few minutes passed. He examined my passport, and then began.

'Mr. France?'

'Yes?'

'What was your reason for visiting Azerbaijan?'

'I'm just a tourist. I've been travelling all across Asia.'

'You are a British national?'

'Yes?'

'Not Azeri?'

'No.'

With each question, my interrogator scanned my face up and down. 'Do you have friends or family in Azerbaijan?'

'No.'

'Have you ever served in the military, in any country?'

'*No.*'

He rubbed his brow, and tilted his head. 'Have you ever been part of a terrorist group, Mr. France?'

'No, I just climb mountains.'

He replaced his glasses on his forehead, and leant back. 'Tell me, what is your reason for visiting Armenia?'

'Aragats.'

'*Aragats?*' his eyebrows lifted. 'You want to climb the sacred mountain?'

'I'm going to try.'

'Be careful, Mr. France, a storm is on the way.' He stamped and returned my passport. 'Good luck.'

I reached Yerevan with the downpour. Heavy drops of rain tumbled from the menacing sky, riddling my body as I dashed through the flooded streets. All was rendered grey. Distorted faces peered through dark windows and cars sat idle on the roadside. I slipped into a stairwell and shook my head. It was cold in here. The concrete steps wound up five stories of drab 1920's townhouse.

From the top, a soot-stained window offered a glimpse out into the city.

Yerevan is fascinatingly constructed, with two huge concentric circles, parted by gardens, then a grid system within. The centerpiece is a single diagonal thoroughfare which jolts across the entire city, rising on the boundary of the circle up a broad stairway to a viewing platform beyond.

I opened the door into a cramped little hostel. A young lady was sitting in the gloom beside a candle, reading a book.

'Hello, do you work here?'

She raised her finger for fifteen seconds, finished her chapter, closed her book, and stood up to greet me. 'Yes.'

I followed her to a desk with a great old logbook. 'There has been a power cut since the storm arrived. I don't know when it will come back, but you're welcome to stay if you like.'

'Just one night, please, for now.'

I dropped my bags in the dorm room, changed out of my wet clothes and found a group of sheltering travellers in the kitchen. I met a Spanish lady who enjoyed visiting war zones, an American girl infatuated with Chernobyl, and a Korean backpacker who had forgotten where she was. We found good conversation as we hibernated for the evening.

The storm persisted for a second day, after which, I decided to take a chance and aim for the sacred mountain. Aragats is a stratovolcano rising to 4090 metres, making it the highest peak in Armenia. It is often confused with the taller *Ararat*, located just across the Turkish border, but historically claimed by Armenia. Aragats is usually in plain view from Yerevan, but through the lingering fog it remained unseen. I packed my gear for bivouacking, enough food for two days, and set towards the unknown.

I travelled by marshrutka (minibus) to the village of Byurakan. Here, a hundred or so houses are built around a Soviet-Era astronomical observatory. To my disappointment, there were no white-coated scientists or wild-haired professors wandering the streets. Instead, I was greeted by a conservative and curious populace. There were four men drinking tea while tending to a punctured tyre. I passed two tittering children running late for school, and a trio of ladies gossiping at the village bus stop.

The four men offered an animated hello, and a cup of tea. They were gesturing and trying to tell me something. One man pointed at my bag, and another towards the mountain. They tried Armenian, then Russian.

I pointed at myself, 'Russkiy, Nyet,' and shrugged.

They shrugged back. I thanked them for their offer and continued through the village. I shortly came to Byurakan's final outpost: a decrepit convenience store. Beyond this lay a sixteen mile climb of an isolated mountain road to the trailhead proper. As I wandered by, the shopkeeper shuffled out onto the road to meet me. He was a small chap with sausage-like limbs and a spherical head. He had a bushy moustache and a shining bald patch on the top of his crown. I felt I recognized him from a popular jar of bolognese sauce.

'Hello, hello!' He waved his hands. 'Stop, stop!'

Before I knew it, he had escorted me inside his shop, sat me down and given me a cup of tea. He sat opposite me on a box of soft drinks, beside his gurning old friend, while his wife manned the checkout.

Dolmio leant forward. 'You, Aragats?'

'Yes.'

He shook his head, and his friend did the same. 'Aragats, danger. *Whoosh, whoosh,* big avalanche! Today, wind, snow, *brrr.*' He shivered, and so did his friend. 'You, Aragats, today: you-,' he drew his finger across his throat and did a sign of the cross. His friend confirmed this with an assertive nod. 'Aragats, no!'

Dolmio, the final gatekeeper to the sacred mountain, had articulated my niggling doubt. Was Aragats safe, or would going there be a death wish? Still, in this land of the clouds, I had not set eyes on the mountain. Do I continue, or do I abandon my attempt on the word of an old watchman?

Dolmio and his leering chum awaited my reply, but it did not come. I was seized by indecision. The broad, bleak Aragats Massif covers almost a fifth of Armenia, and will soon be perished by the redoubling tempest of this late-winter storm. If I fell from the summit, there may not be another soul around for many miles. A flashback to Azerbaijan: the rocks that dropped beneath my feet, the avalanches that pierced the valleys, and the sopping, slipping snow on the mountain.

Dolmio clapped his hands. He muttered something to his wife, arose, and coiled his finger. 'Come.'

I followed him through a door into the back of his shop, up a stairwell and into a large dining room. I didn't know why he was leading me away. Perhaps if I shadowed him for long enough though, he would make my decision for me. He urged for me to sit. Dolmio then laid out two plates, two forks, two tumblers and a bowl of bread. His circular head disappeared into a cabinet. He returned with a large bottle of Armenian vodka and a mischievous laugh.

Dolmio half-filled each of our glasses, and raised his towards mine. Decision made. I raised my glass. Over the next two hours, Dolmio's wife generously prepared a delicious feast for the two of us. Meanwhile, Dolmio introduced me to his favourite regional spirits, several times, until the old shopkeeper and I were best of friends and Anglo-Armenian relations were bilaterally secured.

At 2pm, I caught a marshrutka back to the larger town of Ashtarak, whereupon I had two options. I could go back to my hostel in Yerevan, or climb another mountain for the sake of redemption or masochism. Filled with Dutch courage, foolishness or otherwise, I chose the latter.

My substitute was the nearby Mount Ara, an extinct volcano and shorter sibling of Aragats, which lies twenty miles to the west. Drunk, I flagged down a taxi and asked the two drivers to take me there. He veered off the highway and through a barren landscape. A dirt road split through bedraggled fields and the outskirts of a gypsy village. Then, a craggy mountainside emerged through the fog.

Where the road faded into the fields, I continued on foot. I made good headway up a long grassy slope. The cliffs on the left portrayed their fiery roots, standing like great columns of oozing lava, frozen in time. In a cave at the foot of these cliffs was a small white chapel, doors locked for the winter months. The crags were separated by an enchanting chasm which opened towards the ancient crater. I pursued the slope northwards, eyeing the shifting skies all the while.

By dusk, I was above the snowline at 2500 metres. My inebriated logic supposed that I should camp around here: I would complete a one-kilometre ridge trek to the summit the next morning. As I gazed south though, I saw the approach of one of the biggest storm fronts I have ever seen. Blackness had invaded from the horizon to heavens. It reared towards the mountain in rumbling billows, beset by almighty forks of lightening. A cautionary chill arrived, sent upon a gale. A beast was coming. I turned north and ran.

21

The slope became a hilltop which dipped into a saddle. I waded through waist-deep snow, then along the sprawling ridgeline. Three claps of thunder bellowed. The foreboding winds brought stinging slices of hail, then a deep black haze. There was no trail to follow; no footsteps through the snow. I ran on, keeping to the ridge, my heavy pack jolting my spine with every step. The crest aimed upwards and right, until the gloom opened to a skeletal steel structure.

There was no time for celebrations or mountaintop bellows. I took three summit shots, and checked my GPS. There was a village five miles to the east, at the distant base of the mountain. I took a bearing, checked it twice, and aimed eastwards.

I was now enveloped by the storm. Cruel thunder cackled all around. A squalling gust shrieked and roared. The mountain dropped onto a snow-swept descent. I used my boots as rudimentary skis; every pace now a long skid downhill. I soon reached a deeper gulley – a stream in the summer perhaps – where saplings danced at either side. I could now descend at pace; the gulley channeling me downwards like a shifting staircase.

Eventually, the gulley fizzled into a broad plateau below the snow. Occasional lightening illumined an undulating pasture, interspersed with silhouettes of stone. I double-checked my bearing, and marched on.

By 9pm, drenched to the flesh, the hailstorm gave way to steeping bouts of rain. I was a mile from the village, when a concrete sanctuary came into view. It was featureless, and without a roof. I crept around the front of the building, and found a half-height opening at ground level. I flashed my head-torch into the cavity, and found a sheltered basement with rubble and scraps of building material on the ground. With little hesitation, I crawled in.

Once inside, the basement was just about tall enough for me to stand. It was watertight, except for a large opening where a stairway ought to belong. Here, rain poured in. There were no signs that any other people, or indeed animals, had used the building recently. It stood dormant and deserted. Biblically, when the great deluge came, and Noah built an ark for the animals of the world, early scriptures tell that *'There is a great mountain in Armenia,'* and that, '*the ark came to shore upon the top of it.*' Like Noah and his creatures, I too had found my refuge upon the mountain.

I first barricaded the door, wary that wolves prowl these highlands, before hanging my wet clothes out to dry. I unraveled my mat and sleeping bag and lay down in my dismal abode. I could do nothing now but lie and listen to a raindrop symphony: outside, rain sandblasted the stiff concrete walls, like rippling rounds of machine-gun fire. On the open floor above me, rain slapped into bulging puddles, as though I had a neighbour upstairs, running himself a bath. Then, down in my dingy basement, there was a fulsome splash, as a swollen droplet dripped, sending an echo around my chamber.

All I could hear was the rain like so, until something scuttled past my head. I flashed my torch, and found a little mouse peering at me from behind my rucksack. I smiled at him, but his beady eyes did not waver. I could hardly blame him for seeking shelter too, on such a miserable evening, but I clapped my hands, until he dashed across the basement and back out into the downpour. Poor fellow.

I was warm in my sleeping bag, and I enjoyed spending time with my thoughts. I sent Dolmio my distant thanks, as I wondered what I might have endured had he not turned me from the great Mount Aragats. The storm did not relent until the early hours of the morning. The skies had been cast so murky, I doubted that light could ever find them again. But then, at dawn, an ethereal sunbeam fractured the residual cloud. The pastures sparkled with a green and dazzling glow, and the tree-lined buttresses of Mount Ara stood firm once more.

I packed my bag, got dressed into my dampened boots and clothes, and then passed a young shepherd and his stock on my way to the roadside. I said 'Hello.' The boy returned with a bewildered glance.

Although Aragats, my destined mountain, remained unclimbed and unseen, I was glad to have detoured into Armenia. The wild storm provided more than a dose of fear, bringing detox, precious solitude and a new-found awe for the power of the mountains.

I outstretched my arm to the first vehicle I saw, and asked of the smart gentleman within, 'Yerevan?'

'Yes,' he replied.

The next day, I was back in Georgia, travelling north of Tbilisi at sundown. On the word of a Slovakian traveller in Bishkek,

I was aiming for a skiing village in the heart of the Caucasus, named Gudauri. He told me of a backpacker oasis, surrounded by towering snowcapped mountains, but, he warned me, 'Don't go there too late in the year, or Gudauri might be deserted.'

Sitting up top in a rusting marshrutka, I was the de facto driver's mate, charged with gathering bus fees from the passengers and returning their change. I rather enjoyed this chore, having practised it in Central Asia. For a blip of time, I was a working cog in a quirk of local life. For the driver, an esteemed subordinate. For the passengers, a trusted middleman. Yes, somebody may take my place when I leave, and yes, they may not drop coins between the seats, and may understand the convoluted pricing structure, but would they, many months after that time, look back and think to themselves, '*I grabbed that job by the testes and made it my own,*'? Probably not.

Accordingly satisfied, I hopped off the marshrutka in Gudauri and gave the driver a discerning nod. What ensued would be my second reenactment of Mary and Joseph's hapless search for a birthing shelter, except this time Mary was at a full moon party in Thailand. So, now just a wifeless carpenter, I followed the distant glow of an illuminated hostel sign, and knocked on the door of my first inn.

'Zdravst, [Hello],' said an aproned lady holding a bunch of parsley.

'Zdravst. Can I stay for two nights?'

She spared me a sympathetic gaze. It was dark outside, and Gudauri is miles from anywhere. The lady disappeared, argued with her son, abandoned her parsley, and returned with a 'No.' The hostel was closing for the summer tomorrow morning.

The second hostel was chained at the gates, as was the third. One hostel remained in this ghost town, sited along an unlit track far from the roadside. It was a tall, square building of three stories. There were a couple of lights on inside, and one gate remained ajar. I pushed through onto the driveway, and paused by the front door. Within: chattering, footsteps, and creaking floorboards. The footsteps approached, and before I could knock, the door swung open. I faced a mountain man, with dark hair, dark stubble, ropes on his shoulders, weather-beaten clothes and stiff climbing boots. He frowned at me.

'Hello,' I said, 'Is your hostel still open? I'm sorry if I'm intruding.'

He scratched his beard and sloped his head. 'The hostel is closed. It's the end of the season. My friends and I have just returned from a seven-day ski tour. Tonight, we are having a private party.'

'I see.' I stepped back.

'So you must join us! Georgians never turn away a guest. Come. My name is Anton.' He led me into the enveloping warmth of his pine-clad hostel. Up a pair of staircases was a brightly painted den, scattered with beanbags, posters and reams of outdoor gear, and filled with an unwashed musk. Here, Anton introduced me to his friends, and said we would shortly reconvene for a traditional dinner.

'Hi,' said a tall, curly-haired young man. 'My name is Balu.'

'You mean, like the-.'

'Yeah, the bear in *The Jungle Book*: Balu.'

'Ah, my name's Oli.'

'I'm from Hungary, and this is Portyanko, from Moscow.'

I shook hands with another curly-haired man, with bright eyes and a curvaceous face.

We chatted for a while, before being summoned towards the scent of a Georgian feast. A table built for ten was surrounded by sixteen. Amongst us, two giant platters of sizzling shashlik, two enormous bowls of salad, great piles of bread, dishes of steamed dumplings, sauces of chili, walnut and herbs and three jugs of Georgian red wine. No music nor entertainment was needed, for Anton stood at the head of the table, wine in hand, and began his toast. I have no clue what he said, but for five minutes, his guests howled with laughter, glugged red wine and drummed on the table.

The banquet lasted for three hours or more, with toasts from around the table interspersing endless courses of food. By the end, we all linked arms and swayed as my new friends taught me a Russian song. A soprano from Moscow with bright red hair led the melody, which seemed one of joy and laughter. But when I asked Portyanko what it was about, he replied with a titter, 'Slaves!'

Later, we gathered outside around a roaring campfire. I sat beside Anton, Balu and Portyanko, and we talked about my journey.

'Tomorrow,' said Anton, 'when you go into the mountains, you must be careful not to climb on the western side of the valley. If you do, you could end up in South Ossetia. It's very risky to cross this border without permission from Georgia. Stay on the eastern side of the valley.'

'Do you have any suggestions?'

'Ah, yes. There's a mountain you can climb from the doorstep of our hostel, *Chrdili*, marked by a giant crucifix on the summit. This is the mountain that made me fall in love with Gudauri.'

'So, Oli,' said Balu, 'where will you go after Georgia?'

'I'll continue into Turkey, stop in the Kackar mountains, and then travel along the coast of the Black Sea and into Istanbul. From there, I will return home.'

Portyanko, who had enjoyed more helpings of wine than most, swirled his head towards us. 'I've been to Istanbul once, yes, but it was a mistake. I was partying in Moscow, then I woke up naked in a hostel in Istanbul with only my passport, a toothbrush and-, and a spoon.'

Anton roared, 'It's true!'

The next day, no gloom, no fog, no rain, no wind, no greyness. A brief haze from the night before, perhaps, but that was soon cured by Gudauri's invigorating air. I packed light, taking only an extra layer, my crampons, and some food and water. I set out under sapphire skies, caressed by wanderlust fluffy clouds of the imagination.

I trekked back along the dirt road, across a small farmer's field, then up a hillside and onto a rolling ridge. On the southern side of this ridge, specks of springtime greenery probed through the melting snow. On the north, accumulated snow drifts hugged the mountainside. I was struck by the stillness I found here. Not the slightest flicker of wind found my face, and the valley-bottom road was only scarcely touched by cars aiming for the Russian border.

I lost all measure and interest in time as I rambled the rolling ridge. Eventually, the crucifix came into view upon a distant crest. I strode towards it with bold, energised steps, until it towered over me. Here, I kicked a seat into the snow, and settled for a while. I gazed over the village, where few locals wandered, and up onto the ski slopes, carved by a handful of snowboarders, then back into the skies, where a paraglider sailed overhead. I waved at him, and he nodded down at me.

This was nothing but a fine day in the mountains. I understood why Chrdili Peak (2504m) had so infatuated Anton with this utopia in the Caucasus.

That evening, I joined Anton and his friends in a night-long torture session, also known as a Russian bath. After being forced to wear a ridiculous pointed felt hat, we were shuffled into Dante's inferno; a hot box of steam exceeding 80°C. As I reached the brink of rigor mortis, I was sent out into the second torture chamber, and instructed to pull a rope. Doing so upturned a bucket of ice-cold water which made my nipples twitch. The process continued like so, stepping between ice and fire for three long hours, until I'd lost half my bodyweight in sweat. The anguish was periodically worsened by a nappy-wearing Jesus-lookalike. He ordered me to stand near naked among my watching friends while he flogged me with a eucalyptus bush.

I finally emerged, an emaciated skeleton about to be liberated of my inflaming skin. I asked Anton whether there was a benefit to the suffering I had just endured.

'Yes,' he replied, 'the Russian bath is a great detox. It removes all that is bad from your body.'

That being the case, I must be the evilest bastard on the planet, because nothing but bones remained.

I said goodbye to Anton and his friends the next morning, thanking them for their generosity. A marshrutka took me south to Tbilisi, then directly west towards the Black Sea. Across the Turkish border are the wild Kackar Mountains. There, I would climb my final mountain, before crossing towards Istanbul, then home and Emma at last.

I arrived in the affluent seaside city of Batumi. This is Georgia's boomtown, of palm-fringed beaches where dolphins glide, of glistening skyscrapers, of picturesque stone boulevards, of coastal mansions, of gardens, of waterways, of wealth. House prices here have tripled in a decade, and the city has started to attract international musicians, along with the region's holidaying tycoons. I might have arrived on the Californian coast, or in the Cote D'Azur.

I checked-in to a cool little hostel, whose reception area looked like the deck of an extravagant yacht, with a gleaming white desk, neat wooden panelling and flashes of chrome. It seemed too smart a place for a bedraggled traveller like me, with the earthy scent of the mountains in my clothes. I handed my passport to an elongated fellow with a young face and a pressed white shirt. I saw the glimmer of his name badge: *Davit*. Davit was courteous at first, sitting with a timid smile, but the following morning, he set about expelling my kind of riff-raff from his establishment.

'Are you going to pay now?' he asked, confronting me in the kitchen.

'Yeah, sure.' I checked my wallet. 'I just need to get some cash.'

He laughed, 'No, no, no. I know what you do.'

'What are you talking about?'

'You go to hostels, but you never pay them. We have had a phone call. You are not leaving here until you've paid.'

I exhaled at the absurdity of what I was hearing.

'See, you're smiling. You know what I mean! You need to pay now, mister.'

'If you want any money from me, I'll be back in ten minutes.'

'Fine,' he spun on his heels, 'then I'm calling the police.'

The great lanky blundering buffoon! I chased after him and slapped my hand on his desk as he lifted the phone. 'Who told you that I'm some kind of thief?'

'Another hostel in Georgia. They warned us about you. You're English, yes?'

'*Yes.*'

'And you've got blonde hair and a beard. Ah-ha!'

It was almost comical, I wanted to grab him by the shoulders and give him a shake. 'Which hostel? I've used two in Georgia. One in Tbilisi, another in Gudauri. I paid at both. Tell me which hostel?'

'No,' he shook his head.

'Call them back right now. I won't be falsely accused for something I did not do.'

Davit's colleague emerged from the kitchen, a portly blonde-haired lady with a squashed face. They had a brief discussion, and Davit agreed to call back the hostel. They talked for a time in Georgian, Davit looking between my passport and me, before he hung up the phone and his cheeks went red.

'It's ok, it's ok.'

'What do you mean? Do you believe me now?'

'Yes, it was a mistake.'

I turned and left the hostel, withdrew some money, returned and placed some of it on Davit's desk, then grabbed my bags and departed. I made it to the street corner, before someone shouted. 'Mr. France, Stop!'

I turned to see a shaven-headed man in a leather jacket

staring at me. He had just climbed out of shining black car in front of the hostel. 'Are you Mr. France?'

'Yes.'

'I would like to talk to you.'

'Who are you?' *Undercover police? Mafia hitman?*

'This is my hostel. I'm the owner.'

I ambled back towards him, scowling slightly, and feeling bitter.

'Sir,' he began, as I stopped two paces before him, 'let me apologise. There has been some confusion. In Georgia, honour among men is very important. I am very sorry that we have questioned *your* honour. You were due to spend two nights here, yes?'

I nodded.

'Then the second night is free, if you still wish to stay. I also have a restaurant in Batumi. Your evening meal is on me.' He extended his hand, and I shook it. No self-respecting backpacker can reject a freebie.

I had travelled across Asia to the brink of my finish line. Now, after mixing with scammers, crooks, chancers, interrogators, extortionists and spies, was Davit, the pre-pubescent beanpole, one final unassuming test for me? When travelling solo, one must learn to fight one's own corner, to become a fierce protector of one's self and one's safety. Sharks, though rarely encountered, will whiff out and feed upon weakness. Most lurk in plain view, fins above the water. Others glide almost imperceptibly along. Tonight then felt like a minor victory; a token to say '*well done,*' for piloting an ordinary lad from Wigan so far across a great continent and through so many ordeals. So, I dined on three divine courses of complimentary fare, satisfied, nervous, excited; knowing that this lad's grand adventure was now *almost* at an end.

22

I traversed the Black Sea with a troop of cigarette-smuggling grannies who whooped as we made it through the border. Eight hundred miles lay between myself and Istanbul. One final country. One last summit.

It was now mid-April. The slopes which rose from the purple waters were freshly coated in wildflowers and verdant tussocks of grass. White-tipped peaks swelled like breaking waves in the far distance, offering my first glimpse of the Kackar Mountains. Although I was getting closer to home, these highlands of eastern Turkey looked as wild as any I have visited so far.

I arrived in the small town of Ardesen, and from there travelled thirty miles south into the mountains, and to the village of Ayder. Here, colourful buildings cling to the hillside above a steep and roaring gorge, lounging locals await the change of seasons, and herds of emaciated cattle ply the precipitous fields. A kebab-frying chef whistled as I wandered by, before a young boy skidded past on a rusting bicycle. There was an old lady filling bottles at the communal spring, and a shopkeeper rearranging his wares. There was a quietness to this town, but it also held a certain charm. There was a purity to the air here. It seemed to drift from upriver, where the valley twists towards the white emptiness that lingers beyond winter.

'Careful,' had said the grocer in Ardesen, 'avalanches in the Kackar.'

Yet these dangerous peaks were luring me forward. Month after month, layer upon layer of copious snow had settled here like an invading army in an untamed land. Droplets of the Black Sea, stolen from the waters, sucked into the air, crystalised, and sent down upon the mountains, were resolute in their new place. Now these frozen droplets took many forms, some crunchy, some moist, some shimmering, others dull, some melting, some hardening, some blue, some grey, some slippery, some rigid. The form of these snowdrops is so boundless that the expansive English dictionary might have offered more than one solitary word to describe them; snow.

I left one bag with an innkeeper in Ayder, and told him I would return the following day. He frowned at me; an expression which I read as caution. I walked less than a mile before I stopped in awe.

Like the grocer suggested, the white army of the mountains had begun its seaward migration. On the mountain road ahead of me lay the remnants of a monumental avalanche. It had tumbled from the opposing valley wall, across the deep gorge, and even up across the road and beyond. The snow stood near forty metres deep and around three-hundred metres wide, like a great silver wall, guarding the Kackar from any trespassers. Its stature veiled the mountainous horizon, leaving me with an unclear sense of what lay beyond.

Indeed, there *was* little beyond here and the village of Ayder, except rock, ice and occasional pine forests. Little, apart from the curious mountain hamlet of Asagi Kavrun. This village lies five miles further along the valley, and would be the base of my Turkish mountain climb. It is an ancestral heartland of the mysterious Hemshin people; bagpipe-playing beekeepers whose legendary mountain castle remains undiscovered.

Seven-hundred years ago, Het'um the Historian, a 14th century Armenian Nobleman, journeyed here, and recounted what follows:

'There is a miraculous and strange place ... which—had I not seen it with my own eyes—I would neither dare to speak about it nor to believe in it. ... There is a district named Hamshen in that area, its circumference being a three day's journey. And despite the district's extent, the place is so foggy and dark that no one can see anything. For no road goes through it. People in those parts say that one frequently hears the sounds of men bellowing, of cocks crowing, of horses neighing in the forest, and the murmuring of a river which flows thence. These are all regarded as trustworthy signs that a settlement of people exists in the area.'

Could they? I asked myself. Could people truly reside past this wall of ice and somewhere in the mountains' great expanse? Could my trek become an exploration of a tempting, cryptic society? I hoped so.

I scrambled over the avalanche debris and along the valley. Deep, boggy snow coated the trail, and no footprints lay ahead of me. I crossed a glacial river, whose icy fringes were melting by the drop, then up a winding track. I saw man-made beehives tucked into the surrounding forest, and a concealed wooden structure, possibly used for hunting. The surrounding mountainsides all showed evidence of recent avalanches: hefty chunks of snow lay strewn along widening chutes. As the afternoon gave way to a clouded dusk, I spied a village in the distance. It lay at the base of a deep valley, where mountains lurched at either side towards the heart of the Kackar beyond.

The buildings drew near across the skyline, until I found myself in the centre of Asagi Kavrun. Around me stood twenty sun-bleached wooden houses built upon bulging foundations of stone. Some houses were submerged in deep snowdrifts, and all of them were completely silent. No smoke rose from the chimneys, and most of the windows were shuttered. Still, there were no footprints in the snow. A squalling rush of wind made the buildings creak. Then, silence resumed. *Where was everybody?*

I crept through the village, spying around the shadows, the deserted animal pens and the lifeless porches. Sometimes I called out, but it was futile. A shrieking gust whistled by a house on the edge of the village. One of the windows was smashed open. I stole towards it through the snow. It was dark inside. There were no signs of activity. I retrieved my head torch and flashed it through the hole in the glass.

There I saw a pile of logs, an axe, a shovel, some rags, a chair hanging from the wall, a beaten old pair of shoes, and a small door which was slightly ajar.

'Hello,' I said, flashing my light into the next room.

Nobody replied.

A chill licked my neck as I leant away. The cold of night was coming. I turned my back on Asagi Kavrun, after giving it a final glance. A few hundred yards to the west lay the base of the gorge, and a fractured snow bridge across a churning river. Beyond that, the snow-plastered face of my destined mountain, Bestas Tepesi. I dashed across the snow bridge on the sound of an unsettling fissure, then climbed to the edge of a gloomy pine forest and set camp.

Darkness fell, but a bright moon illuminated the mountains. I was now cocooned in my sleeping bag under the shade of a lurching tree. My stomach ached from the cold meat kebab I'd been saving since Ardesen. So I lay yearning rest. Tomorrow would begin with an alpine start.

Sleep, though, proved elusive.

Far below my feet, Agasi Kavrun glistened in the moonlight. Its wooden houses, oddly positioned across the empty basin, remained unlit and unfrequented. *Where were* the bagpipers and the beekeepers, the shepherds and the farmers? Had they left for the winter, and if so, to where? Evaporated, migrated, or, as Het'um divined, had they withdrawn into the forest?

I had heard it for a while. A panting, trudging sound from nearby, like a grazing bear. One moment it seemed close, the next, the noise vanished altogether. The sound returned. It *was* a bear, I was sure. They roam the Kackar with wolves. I fetched my ice axe and turned my head towards the forest. Could it see me? Was it watching? Snuffling and shuffling: the echoes so clear.

'Hey! Hey!' I shouted.

I left my sleeping bag and slipped my bare feet into my cold boots. I wore only my underwear, but I pulled on a jacket. It was freezing. I tied my food to a tree one-hundred yards away, and returned with two-armfuls of branches. I used the larger ones to construct a barricade around my camp, then began trying to light some sodden tinder to start a campfire. Nothing would take. I tried and tried until my fingers were charred and my lighter ran out of fuel. Then I paused. I heard the snuffling sound again. But was it coming from the nearby stream? Or was it the lick of wind against the pine needles? Was the bear a delusion?

I slumped in my sleeping bag, ice axe lodged in my unyielding grip, wondering if I was losing my mind. I gazed across to my barricade and snorted; there's no way it would stop a three-hundred-kilogram bear, fresh out of hibernation. I may as well lay back and accept my fate. Anyway, perhaps the Hemshin people would come and save me.

Through the night, my mind flitted between dream and hallucination, each as indistinct and uncertain as the other. Dawn was two hours away when, mercifully, my alarm began to ring. Within a few minutes I was dressed and ready to climb the mountain.

I took only the essentials I would need, leaving most of my gear at camp. Bestas Tepesi (2930m) was just an eight-hundred metre climb away, but the snow had barely hardened overnight, and the avalanche danger brought continued paranoia. There was no trail up the mountain, just a series of bulging mounds, gullies, boulders and small cliffs, all coated in several feet of snow.

I made good progress along a broad mound, before crossing the avalanche-battered base of a wide ravine. My nose took me up a steep slope beside a sparse cluster of trees, some of which had been destroyed by cascading snow. I pursued a larger mound next, with more energy, more adrenaline. It was steeper and more exposed. The snow beneath my feet slipped with every step, sometimes sending a wash of debris down below my footsteps. The further I climbed, the more I committed to the mountain, for with every forward step, one must take another step to return. But I had not journeyed to a ghost town, nor fended off an imaginary beast for nothing.

By 7am, I broke through a short cornice and onto to the plateaued summit ridge. The dawn sun burned through the twilight cloud. Snowdrops sparkled about my feet, and myriad summits rose from the horizon lit by the golden shafts of daybreak. I felt invigorated. I had climbed four mountains, in four countries, in twelve days, and as I marched to the mountaintop I was struck by a twinge of emotion. My journey, designed by a dream, planned on a whim, was almost at an end. All that remained was to escape the clutches of these enchanting mountains, and travel to Istanbul.

On my descent, I employed not a moment's hesitation. My west-facing slope was awakened by the climbing sun and all the snow went soft. I skipped, skidded and swept downhill, rescuing my food from up a tree along the way. To my relief, my possessions at camp had not been mauled by a ravenous bear. I packed my things, dashed across the weakening snow bridge and returned to the peculiar village of Asagi Kavrun.

I smiled at the houses. Whatever secrets this village held remained undiscovered by me; its people and its customs *still* only as broad as my imagination. To my surprise, though, as I retraced my footprints towards civilisation, I saw a figure approaching along the trail.

She came on skis, steam rising from her back into the cold air. She wore a rucksack and expensive sports clothing, and she stopped as she reached my side. The lady lifted her luminous sunglasses onto her forehead. 'I had heard there was solo walker in the valley.'

'*Had you?*' I replied.

'Yes, somebody saw you yesterday.' I frowned; the words made me feel uneasy. 'I was worried about you,' she continued, 'there are so many avalanches at this time of year. Did you spend the night?'

'Yes, across the gorge, below Bestas Tepesi.'

'You're a lucky man. Not many people go into the Kackar in winter. Anyway,' she replaced her glasses and dug her ski poles into the ground, 'see you around.'

'Wait,' I replied, 'who was it that saw me yesterday?'

'Ah,' she smiled, 'the local people are always watchful.'

The lady kicked forward and skied off along the valley.

I reached the village of Ayder shortly after midday. The Kackar mountains had left a profound impression on me, and like most of the mountain ranges I have explored, have so seduced my intrigue that I feel my return is inevitable, one day.

That evening, I met a jolly bunch of old men beside the whistling kebab chef. After summoning me over for an impromptu traditional dance, the men invited me into their restaurant. They insisted that my lavish dinner was a gift.

Then, the next morning, I waited for two hours on the roadside until a trundling minibus stopped to take me to the coast. I travelled to Ardensen, then to Rize, then along the Black Sea to the industrial city of Trabzon. My finish line was nearing. My trail suddenly felt different: hot, bright, and more familiar. Europe was truly nigh. The busboy sprinted across the station in Trabzon to secure me a seat on the day's last bus for Istanbul.

This was it; the final leg of my journey across the mountainous spine of Asia. A journey which has taken me through eleven countries, to the summit of fourteen mountains, across a distance of eight-thousand miles, and along the span of one-hundred-and-eight days. This sixteen-hour overnight bus ride would deliver me to Asia's final outpost, unscathed, alive and supremely fulfilled.

I departed the bus and opted to walk the last stretch across the bridge into Europe. Daybreak arrived as the thunder of a mega-city echoed all around. The bronze minarets of Istanbul were my first sight of a new continent. I joined a throng of fishermen across the bridge into Europe and paused a while above the river.

I felt I ought to do something: begin cheering, high-five some strangers, or call home and let tears splash my cheeks. But, in understated British fashion, I stopped in a quiet spot and unfurled a pocket-map of Istanbul, whereupon I realised that I was on the wrong bridge. I'd crossed into Europe an hour ago, when I was sleeping on the bus with dribble down my chin. But it didn't really matter; I had made it.

23

Three Months Later.

I stood alone. Flecks of light flashed by as the sun plied a course through drifting clouds. I whiffed the scent of burning candles, and listened to an excited but reverent chatter from behind. I lifted my gaze to the lofty beams which rose above me, and remembered the journey that had brought me here.

It began with tedium, and the other common snares of modern life. I might have changed career, but my heart drew me elsewhere. I sought sanctuary on the familiar wanderlust path; the path that I knew so well, on which I hung the promise of salvation. If this sounds dramatic, it is intended to. Life rushes by in an incredible flash. To lack joy in life is to waste life itself. And such was my thirst for stimulation, for excitement, for adrenaline, for a life-lifting experience, that I could not subdue my urge for adventure; the most potent medicine I knew. I *needed* to go, truly and irresistibly.

This does not mean, however, that I had no doubts about doing so. These were threefold. First; that my adventure would be only a fleeting fix for my complex grievance. Second; that my endeavours would not provide *any* of the exhilaration I yearned for. Third; that my disappearance, amid a house renovation and a forthcoming wedding, was downright ignoble and selfish. I considered, as I stood there among the smoking candles, whether I had found what I was looking for as a result of my journey, and whether, indeed, it was all worth it.

Solitude. This was the essential ingredient. Had I travelled in a pair, I would only have needed to solve half as many problems. My motive to engage with strangers, if merely to wiggle my tongue and emit a few syllables, would have been diminished. As would my liberty to act on a whim; to be, simply, *adventurous*. Solitude was invaluable.

Reason. The basis for my journey was to rediscover a contented state. I knew that being out in the world was good; *that it was doing me good*, that it was challenging me, allowing me to grow and allowing me to confront the mettle which resides among my flesh and bones. It gave me comfort during my ordeals – being detained in Uzbekistan, lost in a land-mined jungle, interrogated, spied upon and skirted by avalanches – that they were nurturing a more robust, resilient version of myself.

Objective. This gave my journey validation. Tracing the mountainous spine of Asia, climbing mountains of ice, rock, jungle and scree, seeking obscure villages in the remotest corners of the earth; all these things leant direction to a confused mind. These objectives gave me purpose. They became my driving force, my obsession, my stimulus to strive onto mountaintops and pursue the lesser-trodden trail towards the west. Then, when it was all over, completing these objectives made the journey the greatest achievement of my life.

As for happiness, the holy grail, finding this was left open to chance. The foundations stood to let it prosper – solitude, reason and objective – and I yearned for it to happen. Yet nothing guarantees this emotion, even mountains, as I had found. It *could* have transpired that I wasted four months traipsing across a continent feeling every bit as miserable as I did flogging kitchens.

Instead, and to help happiness along, I developed a mantra: *my mind is my entity*, an object under my dominion. I have the power to control it. My mind *will* try to run free, to settle in unwanted moods and to react to external forces, but why should I let it do so? I can control my limbs, my lungs, my eyes, my mouth. Can I not also control my mind?

I fought against negativity when it arose, and hardship when it came. I felt the gradual swell of joy rise within me like precious rains in a drought. And as I opened myself to the world, the world replied with warmth, humility, kindness, captivation, and all the enlivening challenges I yearned for. The world gave boundless happiness; enough for a lifetime and more. What began as an adventure, became an awakening.

One question, though, remains. Was my journey still just a selfish foray? Emma had said to me before my departure, 'I would rather you go and be happy, than stay and be miserable.' She granted me time to wander, and through wandering I found direction. I re-established my life's purpose and discovered that paradise, happiness, euphoria, or whatever it might be called, is as much a state of mind, as a place on earth. With this revelation, I am more complete. I am more content. I am a better person to be around. I have resolved any frustration or regret before venturing on into married life. On the question of selfishness then, only *you*, dear reader, can really answer that. For me, though, only one thing awaited.

The organ chimed with Elgar's Nimrod. The chatter fell silent. Emma took twenty paces towards my side and lifted her sparkling veil. My quest for happiness was complete.

Dear Reader,

Thank you for purchasing and taking the time to read my book. I hope you enjoyed the story I told of my Asian adventure. If so, I have one small favour to ask. As a self-published author, the success of my work relies hugely on reader word-of-mouth. If you could recommend this book to a friend, give it a mention on social media, or write a review on Amazon (or even help with all three!), I would be immensely grateful. Additionally, please feel free to contact me with any thoughts. I would love to hear from you.

Thank you once again, and happy adventuring!

Oli

www.oliverfrance.com

About the Author

Born and raised in Wigan, England, Oli France graduated in Outdoor Leadership from the University of Central Lancashire. He is a qualified British Mountain Leader who has travelled to almost fifty countries (and counting!). Oli earns a living leading expeditions around the world, and occasionally by writing and talking about his adventures. Head to Oli's website (**www.oliverfrance.com**) for more information, and for links to his social media channels.

Printed in Great Britain
by Amazon